*To Durga,
my ama yoga teacher
Namaste,
Lindy*

# Tales from the Crepe

## and other stories

by

## Lindy Stebbins

Copyright 2017 ~ Linda Campbell Stebbins
ISBN: 10: 1544829302

~

*"It's time for Mrs. Phuddle*
*We hope that you like trouble!*

*It's time for Mrs. Phuddle*
*And we hope that you're insured!"*

~

Lisa's song
Circa 1980-85




Cover art by Lisa Hillary Ryan

# Tales from the Crepe

# Tales from the Crepe

## Table of Contents

| | |
|---|---|
| Stepford Pies | 1 |
| The Silence of the Jams | 7 |
| The Icing on the Wall | 12 |
| The Purple Pie Eater | 18 |
| The Whining | 24 |
| The Haunted Fritters | 28 |
| Devil's Food Graveyard | 32 |
| Drear Window | 38 |
| The Glob | 44 |
| The Bread Zone | 49 |
| The Beets Motel or "Sicko" | 53 |
| The Ladyfinger Vanishes | 67 |
| A Gathering of Cupcakes | 73 |
| The Poundcake of the Baskervilles | 79 |
| The Hills Have Pies | 83 |
| Nightmare Kitchen | 88 |
| Fry Day, the 13th | 92 |
| The Black Cat Cake | 97 |
| Crepe Show | 101 |
| The Bling | 109 |
| The Tell-Tale Tart | 114 |
| Night of the Living Bread | 118 |
| The Shuddering Jello Mold | 123 |
| The Fudge | 126 |
| Mrs. Phuddle, Cake Whisperer | 131 |

## And other stories

| | |
|---|---|
| Mrs. Phuddle's Extreme Makeover | 136 |
| Mrs. Phuddle Thinks She Can Dance | 145 |
| Mrs. Phuddle, Voted Off the Island? | 148 |
| The Ghost of Downtown Blabby | 156 |
| Mrs. Phuddle's Gothic Nightmare | 164 |
| An Evening of Literary Despair at Viola Turgid's | 174 |
| A Second Evening of Literary Despair | 178 |
| Mrs. Phuddle Strikes a Match | 187 |
| Mrs. Phuddle's Celebration Dinners | 195 |
| | |
| A Note from Lindy | 201 |

# Stepford Pies

Mrs. Phuddle tutted as she eyed the pies on display at Doodleburg's Annual Arts and Crafts Fair. There were twelve entries altogether, each vying for the coveted First Prize ribbon.

Clarissa Snortspoon, she of the Botoxed cheeks, had entered a cherry pie so obviously store-bought it may as well have been barcoded. Mrs. Phuddle just knew that the judges, whoever they were, would not be fooled by Clarissa's perfectly fluted crust.

"Harrumph," Mrs. Phuddle grumbled, and moved on.

The judging would begin in 15 minutes, giving Mrs. Phuddle, whose own entry was a peach pie, ample time to take stock of the competition.

Next in line was a lemon icebox pie that fairly screamed "Pepperidge Farms!" Who were these people and who did they think they were kidding? They certainly were not kidding Mrs. Phuddle.

She glimpsed the name: Viola Turgid.

Mrs. Phuddle chortled discreetly. Dear Viola had even left the lemon icebox pie in its original aluminum pan. Tsk tsk.

Amateur hour.

"Stepford pies," Mrs. Phuddle mused. "That's what they are. Not a real deal in the bunch—except mine, of course."

Lulu Sprockett, Doodleburg's local playwright and patron of the arts, had dared to enter a Baked Alaska, rapidly melting.

Mrs. Phuddle passed it without comment. Why, this wasn't even a pie! Plus Mrs. Phuddle had seen it on display in the freezer section of the Doodleburg Grocery. Brazen tomfoolery!

Mrs. Phuddle allowed herself a smile of pity, and moved on.

Next up was her own glorious peach pie, made from scratch. Only the freshest, juiciest, peaches had made the cut for this pie. Mrs. Phuddle had labored long and hard to get the crust just right. It smelled like heaven. The other pies emanated only a stale, store-bought odor.

In vain did Mrs. Phuddle struggle to suppress a small twerk of superiority. She hoped no one noticed.

The pie pavilion was filling up quickly as the contestants lined up behind their entries presented on the long banquet table. Next came the judges: Myra Tiddlebody, Alfonso Kricket, and Farina Flake.

Farina Flake! Mrs. Phuddle gasped.

This woman knew nothing of cookery! She was notorious for bringing unpalatable dishes to the church potluck dinners. How on earth had she ever been chosen to judge anything edible—let alone anything as grandly edible as a Mrs. Phuddle pie!

Mrs. Phuddle quivered with indignation.

Soon the pavilion was teeming with contest entrants, judges and onlookers, many whom were there to applaud as their family member or friend won one of the prizes: First, Second, and Most Unusual.

One by one the judges sampled the pies, made notes and moved on to the next entry. Farina Flake partook of each pie with gusto—until they reached Mrs. Phuddle's peach pie. Mrs. P observed with confidence as Myra Tiddlebody and Mr. Kricket each took a portion of the marvelous Phuddle peaches. Neither judge could hide their utter delight with such culinary perfection. Their eyes gleamed, they smacked their lips with appreciation, they oohed and aahed.

Then, Farina Flake took a bite—and gagged!

"Blech," Ms. Flake scowled, struggling to swallow. She made a moue of distaste, wiping her mouth vigorously with a napkin.

After that things went a bit grey for our heroine. She barely noticed as the judges moved from pie to pie, tasting and jotting notes. Mrs. Phuddle knew she would win no prize that day. Farina Flake would see to that. As from the bottom of a deep well Mrs. Phuddle heard the judges announce the results of the pie contest.

First Prize: Felicia Flick's bourbon pecan pie

Second Prize: Viola Turgid's lemon icebox pie

Most Unusual:  Lulu Sprockett's Baked Alaska

*But that's not even a pie!* Mrs. Phuddle silently protested.

Coming out of her daze of mortification, Mrs. Phuddle became dimly aware of someone talking to her. It was Viola. She was beaming from ear to pointy ear.

"I can't believe I beat you!" Viola was crowing in a most unseemly manner.

Harsh words of repudiation hovered on Mrs. Phuddle's lips, but she suppressed them, recalling the advice of an old hymn:

*Angry words, oh, let them never
From the tongue unbridled slip.*

Mrs. Phuddle struggled for composure.

"Yes, why, congratulations," Mrs. Phuddle managed to say, her cheeks burning. "I didn't even know you were entering the pie contest!"

Viola nodded. Mrs. Phuddle noticed that her friend's eyes glistened with tears.

"Yep," Viola said. "My dear old Granny Turgid taught me the recipe when I was knee-high to a grasshopper. 'Bout the only thing she taught me that ever stuck."

"Indeed? I never hear you mention this before," Mrs. Phuddle said, wrapping her scorned pie in aluminum foil.

She, at least, would enjoy it!

"Granny tried to teach me how to sew, knit, crochet, and arm wrestle, but I just never caught on. But every time we visited, Granny and I would make a lemon icebox pie. They were so good."

Mrs. Phuddle pursed her lips. She wasn't accusing Viola of prevarication, but surely she was exaggerating, just a bit?

Finally, she just couldn't help herself. "Are you sure you didn't get a little help from Grandma Pepperidge as well?" she prodded.

"What?" Viola's eyes bulged. "What are you implying?"

Mrs. Phuddle mentally kicked herself. How to undo this?

"I'm implying that I'm jealous," she admitted, swallowing her pride. "Also, dying to sample your pie."

After a brief, indignant pause, Viola said, "Certainly," and sliced a piece for Mrs. Phuddle.

Just a small piece.

The pie felt like silk upon the tongue and tasted of fresh lemons and organic cream cheese.

It was quite good.

"Lovely," Mrs. Phuddle declared. "And definitely not a Stepford pie."

Viola shook her head. "Geraldine, you're acting very strange today."

Mrs. Phuddle smiled. "C'mon, let's take our pies over to my place and have a party!"

"I'd like that," Viola agreed.

As they left Mrs. Phuddle spotted Farina Flake at the table, scooping up Lulu Sprockett's Baked Alaska as it melted into a puddle, her cheeks flecked with what one hoped was meringue.

"Most unusual," Mrs. Phuddle murmured, and moved on.

# The Silence of the Jams

For some time now Mrs. Phuddle had been contemplating the silence of the jams. No, not the silence of peach preserves slathered over a hot buttered biscuit (although that was a happy thought). And certainly not the silence of Fredericka and Monika Jams, sisters famous for their collection of bronzed donut holes. Why they collected, bronzed and displayed these on their bric-a-brac shelves was a hot topic of conversation amongst Doodleburgers.

No, it wasn't the silence of those jams, nor those other Jams, that was perplexing Mrs. Phuddle.

Furthermore, the jams she encountered in traffic, tooling around in her 1959 Studebaker, those jams were never silent. Those jams were noisy, indeed. Mrs. Phuddle shuddered, recalling those awful jams, those traffic jams which invariably left her unnerved and in need of strong, dark sweet tea.

As Mrs. Phuddle brewed and baked, sipped and noshed, she continued to contemplate the silence of the jams.

"Tweet?" Fluffy inquired, noting her lady's puzzled demeanor.

Mrs. Phuddle airily waved a hand. "Oh, I'm just contemplating the silence of the jams."

"Tweet tweet?" Fluffy prodded.

Swimmer glanced up from gnawing a rawhide.

"No, not the movie," Mrs. Phuddle replied. "That was *lambs* that were silent. Oh, my, I had nightmares for *years* after seeing that one. Couldn't even look at a dress pattern."

"Tweet?"

"Woof?"

"Yes, you're both right," Mrs. Phuddle agreed. "I should call Dr. Leecher. He was so helpful after my dear Will passed."

"Tweet."

"True, some do call him Leecher the Preacher," Mrs. Phuddle said. "You see, he's a part-time psychiatrist and part-time pastor of United Faiths Online. I hear he does very good work with traumatized alien abductees."

She reached for the phone.

Moments later, having scrolled through a series of menu options ("Press *1 for Donations; Press *2 for Botched Botox; Press *3 for Losing Track of the Kardashians; Press *4 for Donations") Mrs. Phuddle was greeted by a human with a sonorous voice.

"UFO Ministries, Dr. Leecher speaking. How may I heal you?"

"Oh, Dr. Leecher, how wonderful to hear your sonorous voice again! It's Geraldine Phuddle, remember me? You guided me through the deep waters of bereavement many years ago."

From the ensuing silence it was clear that Dr. Leecher did not remember Geraldine Phuddle, until she added, "I baked you all those lemon cream coconut cakes."

"Ah!" Light dawned. "Of course, my dear Geraldine. Tell me," he drawled, "do you still bake?"

"Oh, yes," she said. "In fact, I now own a bakery!"

"Marvelous, marvelous," Leecher the Preacher drooled. "So, tell me, how may I help you this time, my child?"

Mrs. Phuddle bridled a bit at being called "my child," but continued undeterred.

"Dr. Leecher, I have this puzzling, recurring dream about jams," she began.

"Jams?"

"Yes. The silence of the jams."

"Hmm…" Clearly, he was envisioning a series of lemon cream coconut cakes arriving on his doorstep via Feedex.

"You see, my brother Belvedere used to play in a garage band when we were teenagers," she explained. "And they were just awful." She shuddered, remembering. "B.B., as he was known, played the drums. Or, I should say, he banged and crashed the drums."

"Tell me your dream, Clarice," Dr. Leecher rasped.

"Clarice?"

"Er, I mean, Geraldine. What is it about the dream that puzzles you?"

"In these dreams I'm watching B.B. and his pals, Thor and Gunther, playing in the garage. You see, they're having a jam session..."

"Go on..."

"But there's no sound. Their jams are silent. What could this possibly mean?"

"Does this dream frighten you, Clarice?"

Mrs. Phuddle sighed. "Do you even know to whom you're speaking?"

"Ah, yes, I remember. You're running away from the farm, a baby lamb in your arms, and in the distance you can hear the fearful drumming."

"Umm..."

"When can I expect my cake?" Dr. Leecher suddenly demanded.

"I'm sorry," Mrs. Phuddle replied. "But my bakery doesn't mail baked goods. Now, as I was saying..."

"See you in your dreams, Clarice," the doctor murmured, ending the call.

"Dr. Leecher?" Mrs. Phuddle gripped the phone. "Dr. Leecher? Dr. Leecher?"

"Tweet tweet," Fluffy said, which translated, means "Stop this right now."

"Agreed," Mrs. Phuddle said.

She hung up and buttered a biscuit.

# The Icing on the Wall

Mrs. Phuddle awoke with a start. She sat bolt upright in bed, heart racing. Swimmer stirred at her feet, growling deep in his furry throat.

"Tweet?" Fluffy murmured sleepily from her perch.

"Shh, listen."

They listened.

A wail broke the silence: *"The icing on the wall..."*

"What?" Mrs. Phuddle clutched her covers, not wearing her pearls at the moment.

*"The icing on the...waaaall!"*

"Oh, my," Mrs. Phuddle whispered, too terrified to get out of bed and investigate. "Who—or what—is that?"

"Tweet tweet!"

"I don't want to know, either," Mrs. Phuddle quavered. "Go away!" she cried.

Swimmer crawled beneath the bed. Fluffy hid her wee head beneath a wing.

"Good idea," Mrs. Phuddle said, pulling the covers over her head.

This only inflamed the Voice from Beyond.

**"The icing on the wall!"** it thundered.

Mrs. Phuddle huddled within her blanket fortress for hours, too afraid to move. Swimmer whined beneath the bed, his hackles on high alert. Fluffy flew over to nest within the Phuddle tresses, only her beak showing from the depths of fluffy white hair.

*"The icing on the wall,"* the Voice repeated, hissing.

Eventually the Voice grew weaker, sadder. Finally it hushed altogether.

"Just a bad dream," Mrs. Phuddle declared, "or an overactive imagination. Let's go back to sleep, my dears."

Swimmer returned to his place at the foot of the bed, Fluffy to her gilded cage.

They slept late that morning.

Around ten o'clock Mrs. Phuddle padded downstairs for breakfast. She examined the walls for icing. There was only a bit of grease splatter.

"Piffle," she muttered. "I'm making waffles."

Swimmer adored waffles.

But he got kibble. So unfair.

"Frrrr," growled Swimmer.

"Tweet," Fluffy chirped, content with her birdseed.

All was well...

Until bedtime.

Just as Mrs. P and her furries were sailing off on that Good Ship Lollipop, the Voice returned.

*"The icing on the wall!"* it wailed.

"Shush," Mrs. Phuddle grumbled, burrowing beneath her covers.

Swimmer and Fluffy joined her.

Again they spent a night quivering in fear as the Voice wailed for hours.

And again there was no icing on the wall in the morning.

"This has gone on long enough," Mrs. Phuddle declared. "Clearly I am losing my mind and need to see a shrink."

"Tweet?"

"Aroo?"

"Mass hysteria," Mrs. Phuddle replied, dialing Dr. Grindstone.

Once she got her GP on the line, Mrs. Phuddle explained her problem and asked for a referral to a local psychiatrist.

"Unfortunately," Dr. Grindstone said, brimming with kale, "we only have one head doctor left in Doodleburg. Most of them now practice in Whackoma."

Mrs. Phuddle pursed her lips. She did NOT wish to drive on the dreaded I-5 to Whackoma to see anything less than a heart surgeon. "Well, who is the Dooodleburg shrink?"

Dr. G sighed. "Mrs. Phuddle, I'm really loath to recommend this one to you."

"Loath away," Mrs. Phuddle insisted. "I need my head examined in the worst possible way."

"And the worst possible way is how it will be," the doctor replied. "Very well, it's your fun—er—decision."

Mrs. Phuddle made an appointment to see Doodleburg's last remaining psychiatrist that very day. Luckily, he had a cancellation.

Mrs. Phuddle did not heed the warning signs.

At three o'clock that afternoon Mrs. Phuddle was ushered into the rather dingy office of Dr. Frank Lee Pilpoppin.

Mrs. Phuddle thought he seemed vaguely familiar. Where had she seen Dr. Pilpoppin before? He sported a white beard, round gold spectacles, and a three-piece tweed suit. He even brandished an unlit cigar. A memory nagged…

"Freud!" Mrs. Phuddle exclaimed.

"Pilpoppin!" the doctor rejoined. "Please, have a seat, Mrs. Phuddle." He indicated the leather couch, quite slippery. He settled himself into an upholstered wing chair facing her.

"Dr. Grindstone intimated that you were hearing voices?" he prodded as Mrs. Phuddle tried to remain upright on the slick leather couch.

Mrs. Phuddle nodded. "Yes, Dr. Freud..er...Pilpoopin. A Voice from Beyond has awakened me the past two nights."

He chewed on his cigar. "And what does this Voice say?"

Mrs. Phuddle cleared her throat. "Um...it wails something about icing on the wall...over and over for hours."

Dr. Pilpoppin stroked his beard. "That sounds...significant," he intoned.

He was gazing at his own wall, as though it, too, might speak.

Mrs. Phuddle followed his gaze, noticing the certificate hanging there above his desk.

"This...Voice," he ruminated, chewing his cud, "it only comes...to you...at night?"

Mrs. Phuddle wondered if he were going to spit that chewed-up tobacco, but she noticed no spittoon. Surely he wouldn't...swallow? She shuddered at the thought.

From somewhere a bell chimed. His bushy eyebrows shot up, wrinkling his dome. "Pardon me for a moment, Mrs. Phuddle," he said, his cheek bulging. "I must...see to...this."

When he left the inner sanctum, Mrs. Phuddle slid off the couch and crept toward his desk to examine Dr. Pilpoppin's medical certificate.

"The Korry S. Pondence U?" she read. "Oh, dear."

Hearing footsteps approaching, Mrs. Phuddle bustled back to her seat.

"Sorry about the…interruption," the doctor said. Tobacco flaked his beard in an unsavory manner.

He began scribbling onto a prescription pad. "Mrs. Phuddle, I'm writing you a script for Ibax, Xboz, and Vsnooze to alleviate your anxiety, depression, and insomnia."

Mrs. Phuddle knew these meds would not quiet the Voice.

Home again, she ripped the prescription to shreds and tossed the pieces into the trash. "Only one thing to do now," she said to Fluffy and Swimmer. "Appease."

They stared at her with full understanding.

Humming a little tune as she whirred and stirred and mixed the dough, Mrs. Phuddle baked a three-layer caramel cake with thick, creamy icing.

She flung some of it onto the wall.

That night the Voice said, "Thank you."

Thereafter, whenever she baked a cake, Mrs. Phuddle always saved a little icing for the wall.

And the Voice remained satisfied.

# The Purple Pie Eater

Mrs. Phuddle was in her kitchen, baking up a storm. Today she was baking purple pies—Loganberry pies. To be on the safe side, as Loganberries were quite staining, she was wearing two aprons over a faded old housedress.

Fluffy, her wee yellow bird, was staying far away from those purple berries. She didn't want her lovely golden plumage splattered with purple goo.

Swimmer, OTOP, didn't mind purple goo in the least. He was constantly underfoot as Mrs. Phuddle mixed the dough, rolled the dough, and boiled the berries.

"Swimmer, dear, you should be outside," his lady kindly suggested when she almost tripped over him.

She gave him a treat and shooed the happy brown-and-white dog out the back door to the fenced in back yard.

"There you go!" she cooed, shooing him.

Swimmer scarfed his dog cookie, then immediately pressed his wet snout against the glass storm door, tail a-wagging.

"Please let me in, m'lady," his hopeful brown eyes pled. "Let me in so I can stay underfoot while you bake pie!"

But Mrs. Phuddle knew better. He very likely would get splattered with hot Loganberries while tripping her. She was baking six Loganberry pies for the church's fall bazaar, working like a well-oiled pie baking machine.

She hummed a merry tune as she placed two pies into the oven. Two at a time were all she could bake at once. This project was going to take the whole afternoon!

A happy smile brightened her face as she rolled out the dough. She did so love baking.

But her gaze was continuously drawn to little Swimmer, so forlorn as he slobbered against the storm door. How could she be so cruel?

With a heavy sigh she let him in, whereupon he remained underfoot as she placed two unbaked pies onto the kitchen table to await their turn in the oven.

Setting the oven timer, Mrs. Phuddle said, "Come along, dear, into the parlor."

"Tweet?" Fluffy inquired from her perch by the living room window.

"They're coming along nicely, dear," Mrs. Phuddle smiled.

"Tweet tweet," Fluffy yawned, tucking her head for a wee nap.

"Good idea," Mrs. Phuddle murmured, settling comfortably onto the settee. She bunched a pillow beneath her head for a wee nap, too.

Swimmer slumped onto the floor beside his lady, furry head resting on his paws.

The pies in the oven baked.

The pies on the table sat.

The clock on the mantel tick-tocked.

Mrs. Phuddle snored, in a most ladylike manner.

Swimmer raised his head. He sniffed.

He was the only one awake.

Slowly the brown-and-white dog rose to his feet and stre--------etched.

Mrs. Phuddle was dreaming of summers spent in Daisybrook, Georgia, when she was five years old and helping Grandma Butterflut feed the chickens.

"Here, chick, chick, chick," Grandma clucked, spreading chicken feed.

"Here, chip, chip, chip," little Gerry mimicked.

Mrs. Phuddle smiled in her sleep. Even snorted a little bit.

Meanwhile, oh so stealthily, Swimmer was creeping into the kitchen, just to check that everything was okay.

His eyes were twin pools of doggy longing as he gazed upon the two unbaked pies sitting there all undefended upon the table.

But Swimmer knew he wasn't allowed to eat pie. His lady claimed pie was bad for him. Bad! Why, he didn't know. Pie seemed to be awfully good for her!

He snuffled the pies, careful not to bring snout to crust. That was a big no-no!

What's this? Mrs. Phuddle had forgotten to cover the pies with a tea towel, as was her wont, and a nasty fly was buzzing around them!

Swimmer growled at the fly, then snapped his powerful jaws as the pesky critter circled for a landing.

A fly on the pie! This would not do! This was the biggest no-no of all!

The fly buzzed round and round, closer and closer as Swimmer watched with growing concern. When the fly landed upon, shall we say, Pie #2, Swimmer reacted with deadly swiftness.

He slammed a paw upon the fly.

And consequently, upon the pie.

He didn't know why he whomped the fly.

But he smashed the pie.

Swimmer noted (again, swiftly) that his fly-whomping paw was covered in purple goo. Glancing about and espying no witnesses, he licked the paw that whomped the pie.

Oh, my oh my.

He loved the pie.

Swimmer licked the purple paw clean, leaving trace evidence upon his snout.

But what was this?

He heard a buzzzzz.

The fly didn't die!

Swimmer whomped the pie—er, the fly—again and again and again. Soon, he, the kitchen table, the chairs and the floor were splattered with purple goo.

Swimmer licked the table, chairs, floor, and paws in a frenzy to hide the evidence of his crime.

During this frenzied licking, two things occurred: the oven timer dinged, and Mrs. Phuddle awoke.

Yawning and stretching from her nap, she went to the kitchen.

It took her a moment to comprehend the scene—her formerly brown-and-white dog was now a most definite purple. His fur was matted with Loganberries, the floor smeared with purple goo. One of the pies was a total ruin, smashed beyond repair. It quite took her breath away, momentarily.

Regaining her breath, Mrs. Phuddle faced her purple dog.

"Swimmer!" she accused.

The purple dog hung his purple head in shame. The fly buzzed about merrily.

Fluffy flew in from the living room. "Tweet?" she cried, which translated from the Bird, means, "What hath dog wrought?"

Mrs. Phuddle couldn't help but smile. "Behold, the purple pie eater!" she declared, and began to clean up the mess.

The purple pie eater spent the rest of the afternoon in the backyard, far from temptation.

# The Whining

Mrs. Phuddle slammed shut the scary thriller she'd been reading. Whatever had possessed her to read *The Whining* so late at night? She sat within a pool of amber light, so cozy an hour ago, so sinister now. The stairs creaked ominously behind her. Who or what was creeping up to her boudoir?

Swimmer lay at her feet, softly growling in his sleep, as though chasing demon bunny rabbits. What was he dreaming?

Mrs. Phuddle shivered. She placed her book face down on the table, then covered it with a lacy doily. Still, she knew it was there.

*The Whining* told the story of a couple with their two children staying at a rustic B&B in Vermont. The kids didn't like their room—too prissy. They hated the food—too fancy. No mac 'n' cheese. They whined nonstop about decamping to a chain motel and eating at Micky D's.

The Whining, it never stopped, night and day, day and night...

The wind rattled Mrs. Phuddle's windows, startling her.

"Oh, my," she gasped. "I really must get ahold of myself."

"Tweet," Fluffy agreed from her gilded cage.

The hour was quite late, hours past Mrs. Phuddle's regular bedtime, but how could she sleep with *The Whining* shrieking through her head?

"Tweet tweet," Fluffy noted.

"I know, I know, I never should've started reading the dratted book so late," Mrs. Phuddle admitted. "But the plot is so enthralling! You see, this family is stranded at an old Victorian mansion in the mountains during a freak snowstorm. The elderly couple who run the B&B shuffled about like zombies, muttering strange incantations."

"Tweet?"

"Well, they curse The Whining that never ends, never ceases, never stops, night and day, day and night, under the hide of them. When the parents of the br—little darlings confront them about their curses, the old folks just reply, 'the wind…it whines…and whines.'"

Mrs. Phuddle glanced about nervously. "But the parents suspect they really mean the kids who never for a moment stop whining about being stuck in this old Victorian mansion with no Wi-fi. And they find—" Mrs. Phuddle swallowed. "They find a word written in Maalox on their bathroom mirror."

"Tweet tweet?" Fluffy demanded, no longer at ease within her gilded cage.

"STARB." Mrs. Phuddle gulped. "Just those letters. Who knows what that means? It's like they misspelled 'stab' or something…"

"Tweet?"

"Well, yes, there's more, Fluffy. The br—children find this door at the end of a long dark hallway...that pulses..." She took a deep breath. "The door pulses, lie a heartbeat."

"Tweeeet?"

"That's where I stopped reading," Mrs. Phuddle replied, wrapping a fleece blanket about her shoulders. "Where the br—kids were turning the knob on that door...that door with a—gasp—heartbeat."

"TWEEET!" Fluffy cried, which translated from the Bird, means, "Aiieeeehhh!"

"I'm sorry, Fluffy!" Mrs. Phuddle exclaimed. "I'll say no more about it!"

She cast a furtive glance at her own door, the front door, lest it made any untoward throbbings. She flinched when the door began to rattle.

Out there, in the gloom, there came a whining, very similar to Dakota Fanning in *War of the Worlds.* That whining, too, had been endless, unbearable...

Mrs. Phuddle struggled to her feet, casting off fleece. She hobbled to the window, legs trembling, and pulled aside the drapes. A cold November wind was howling, while the street lamp illuminated...

"A freak snowstorm," she whispered.

Swimmer padded to her side, a low whine in his throat. (The Whining was contagious.) Fluffy flew to Mrs. Phuddle's plump shoulder for protection.

"Tweet," Fluffy whined.

"Aroo," Swimmer whined.

"I know what can fix us right up," Mrs. Phuddle declared. "A cookiecism!"

A few minutes later a dozen peanut butter cookies were baking in the Phuddle kitchen, the delicious aroma wafting through the house and dispelling the gloom.

It worked like a charm every time.

# The Haunted Fritters

Mrs. Phuddle awoke one fine November morning with a craving for bacon-grits fritters. As a rule, Mrs. Phuddle enjoyed a bowl of oatmeal with walnuts and blueberries for breakfast, or a kale yogurt smoothie—when no baked goods were available.

There was a time in her life when she made fritters for breakfast every Sunday morning before church—apple fritters, zucchini fritters, banana fritters, savory corn fritters, and best of all—bacon-grits fritters, served with steaming hot coffee from the percolator. One might say she'd been frittering her life away, but then one would be guilty of making a very lame pun.

"Will always liked my bacon-grits fritters best," Mrs. Phuddle recalled with a nostalgic smile. "I'd make six, he'd eat five, leaving one for me. I was much thinner in those days…"

This morning she boiled the grits and stirred in cheese, crumbled bacon bits, and minced onions before rolling the grits into patties and breading them in flour.

"Tweet!" Fluffy remarked as her lady prepared the fritters for frying.

"Oh, yes, Fluffy," Mrs. Phuddle nodded, pausing a mo' to smile in sweet remembrance of things past. "Will enjoyed every kind of fritter, to be sure. But if he caught a whiff of my bacon-grits fritters sizzling in the pan, he'd come a-running."

"Aroo!" Swimmer chimed in, tail wagging.

"Here you go, dear," Mrs. Phuddle said, handing him a dog biscuit.

He trotted happily away with his prize.

Mrs. Phuddle resumed the breading and frying.

"No doubt, if I'd made a dozen fritters, Will would've eaten eleven," she fondly mused.

"Tweet tweet."

Mrs. Phuddle nodded. "Yes, it's a good thing I didn't, or Will would've—"

Her voice caught as she gazed out the window. A cold bright Autumn sun cast a golden glow over the land.

"It will be a lovely day," she murmured.

She removed the first three fritters and drained them on paper towels.

"Tweet?"

"Oh, nothing, Fluffy," Mrs. Phuddle replied, dropping three more fritters into the pan. "I was just going to say it was a good thing for his health that I didn't cook 12 fritters."

She sighed.

"Tweet tweet," Fluffy cooed, fluttering to the Phuddle shoulder to stroke the fine white Phuddle hair.

"But in the end, it really didn't matter…"

Mrs. Phuddle flipped the fritters and when they were done, drained them beside the other three. She really wasn't hungry anymore. A tear splashed her coffee cup.

"He so loved those bacon-grits fritters," Mrs. Phuddle said in a suspiciously shaky voice.

Swimmer trotted to her side and nosed her apron in sympathy, where there were bacon-grits fritter splotches. She patted his head and wiped her tears.

Mrs. Phuddle took her coffee to the living room to read the paper while the six fritters drained, though her eyes didn't scan nor the pages turn. She was lost in memory. Every now and then she muttered, "Oh, flitter," or perhaps she said, "Oh, fritter," but only Mrs. Phuddle knows for sure.

After she finished her coffee Mrs. Phuddle returned to the kitchen to eat a fritter or two.

She gasped. There was only one fritter left.

One fritter.

A shiver ran up her spine. "W-Will, was that you?" she whispered.

Her heart pounded. Had Will's spirit spirited away 5 fritters?

Mrs. Phuddle sank into a kitchen chair.

"Oh, my," she said, clutching her robe where her pearls would be if she were wearing them, only she seldom if ever wore pearls for breakfast. At the moment she really needed those pearls.

She sat there stunned for the longest time, contemplating the lone fritter. She failed to notice the brown-and-white dog crouching beneath the kitchen table, smelling of bacon-grits fritters.

His tummy churning, his belly full.

# Devil's Food Graveyard

"Such bad taste," Viola Turgid, Mrs. Phuddle's dear friend and partner-in-crime, commented as she chewed a fudge brownie.

Mrs. Phuddle pursed her lips. "Indeed," she agreed, surveying the scene in Lulu Sprockett's backyard, garishly decorated for Halloween.

Gauzy ghosts dangled from tree limbs. A panther-sized black cardboard cat crouched on the tumble-down fence, which was festooned with swaths of spidery cobwebs. Skeletons leered from the porch above grinning Jack-o-Lanterns.

"Plastic," Mrs. Phuddle noted, prodding a pumpkin with her toe.

Eerie wails and groans arose from tombstones planted here and there in the dimly lit yard.

"Plastic," Mrs. Phuddle murmured as she examined a gravestone thusly inscribed:

*Frank N. Stein*
*Rest in Pieces*

Platters of chocolate brownies, cupcakes and Halloween candy, including gelatin worms, were scattered about on the plastic monuments.

"Tacky," Viola replied, sampling a Ho-Ho.

The two ladies hovered beneath a dangling plastic spider sporting a human skull. Their disdain wafted about the premises along with the eerie cries.

"Entirely overdone," Mrs. Phuddle said, sipping a murky red beverage she devoutly hoped was tomato juice.

They wandered back to the porch, where they could see their hostess mixing drinks in the kitchen.  They sank gratefully into chairs around a patio table. They had to shout to be heard above the ghostly wails and groans from the speakers.

Mrs. Phuddle set a basket filled with yeast rolls and goat cheese on the table. "Whew, this thing is itchy," she complained, adjusting her Shirley Temple wig.

"You make a very convincing Heidi, Geraldine," Viola said kindly. "I bet it was a beyotch finding lederhosen."

Mrs. Phuddle frowned. "Viola, language," she chided. "But, yes, it was. And this flipping corset is killing me!"  She smoothed down her skirt over the flouncy petticoats that also bedeviled her.

Viola snorted. She hadn't needed a special Halloween costume, as her usual attire served nicely:  a flowing purple caftan, with a green turban on her head, held together with a faux ruby. She had been carrying a pack of Tarot cards as a prop, but mislaid them somewhere amongst the tombstones.

A dozen or so Zombies wandered about the cemetery, along with a Carrie White or two in blood-drenched prom dresses, a smattering of witches, and several vampires. But only one Shirley Temple Heidi.

Mrs. Phuddle spread goat cheese on a butter roll and nibbled. Peering through the gloom of the night, she said, "Isn't that a hand emerging from a grave?"

"Yep," Viola said, snacking on a devil's food cupcake. "Twelve ninety-nine at KRAY-Z-MART."

A vampire with bloody fangs joined them at the table.

"Hello, Lulu," Mrs. Phuddle greeted.

"I vant to dwink your blod," Lulu intoned through her plastic fangs.

Viola rolled her eyes.

Lulu removed her fangs. "How do you like my sound effects?" she asked. "Lordy, those hurt," she said, shoving the fangs away. "I made them myself—the graveyard sounds, not the fangs. Pretty spooky, eh? I wailed, groaned and moaned, even yodeled. I'm thinking of marketing them."

"Your sound effects?" Mrs. Phuddle adjusted her curls. The wig was so tight, hot and itchy she longed to rip it off and stomp on it. "Quite chilling, I'm sure."

"If you ladies will excuse me," Viola said, rising from the table. She headed to the kitchen to pour herself a Bloody Mary.

Sonny and Cher sashayed by, hand in hand, and warbling, "I got you, babe."

"Oh, look," Lulu grinned. "I do believe that's Petulia Goodtimes and Horris Winterspeare, together again."

"Hello, girls," Horris greeted as he and Petulia joined them at the table.

"You make a fetching Cher, Horris," Mrs. Phuddle said.

"Arf arf," Lulu giggled.

"I feel moonstruck tonight," Horris said, caressing his long black wig. "How about Petty? Isn't she a cute little Sonny?"

Sonny stroked her bushy brown mustache.

Viola returned, holding a very large drink. She flopped into a chair, already tipsy from the mere fumes.

"So, who're you s'posed to be?" she asked, slurping her BM. "No, no, don't tell me! Liz and Dick!"

"Cheney?" Petulia replied. She sported a Dutchboy wig with bangs, a furry vest over a paisley blouse, and striped bell-bottom pants. A gold medallion hung around her slender neck.

"Nooo," Viola slurred. "Liz Taylor and Richard Burton, you silly nim—"

"Vie!" Mrs. Phuddle warned.

"Jus' havin' shum fun," Viola retorted.

"We had to plunder the thrift shops to bag these threads," Horris explained. He wore a fringed vest over a purple blouse and stone-washed jeans, held up with a wide red belt. Long loop earrings dangled from his somewhat hairy ears. One of his false eyelashes was askew, and he was a bit over-rouged.

"So, what are ya, then?" Viola persisted, glancing towards the kitchen. Her Mary was running low on blood. "Brad and Angie??" she snickered. "Oh, wait—I mean, obviously you're—hic—Frankenstein and Vampira." She threw back her head and brayed like a banshee.

"Vie, I think we need to go home now," Mrs. Phuddle cautioned.

"Need 'nother drinkie," Viola replied, staggering away.

"Let's groove through the graveyard, babe," Cher suggested, flipping his wig.

"Good idea," Sonny agreed. She flashed the peace sign as they left.

Mrs. Phuddle hissed, "Lulu, I must get Viola home before she's totally dr—inebriated. She's not accustomed to hard liquor, so it goes straight to her head. You just saw it!"

She rose to go, thinking, *Must shred Shirley Temple wig.*

Lulu chortled. "Don't worry, Gerry! Liquor's too expensive! There's nothing in that blender stronger than horseradish."

"You mean—"

Lulu tapped her temple. "Power of suggestion. Viola just thinks she's—" She hushed as Viola careened into their table.

"Having fun, Vie?" Lulu inquired, winking at Mrs. Phuddle.

Viola nodded, sloshing her drink. Her eyes narrowed as she zeroed in on Sonny and Cher wandering amongst the gravestones. "Why'd they leave us? I wanna have a word with little Mish Goodtimes…"

Mrs. Phuddle gripped Viola's bony arm. "Absolutely not, Vie. I'm quite ready to go home!" She nodded to her hostess. "Lovely party, Lulu. Quite authentic."

She prodded Viola, who bellowed, "But I need another round!"

"And I need to go home," Mrs. Phuddle firmly insisted.

She could not endure this dratted mess of curls on her head for another instant. Her skull fairly screamed for sweet release. Mrs. Phuddle trotted to her car with Viola reluctantly trailing behind, grousing and muttering imprecations.

Once in the driver's seat of her 1959 Studebaker, Mrs. Phuddle ripped off the Shirley Temple wig and flung it out the window.

"Aaaiiiieeeeggggh," she cried in relief.

"Lulu should record *that*," Viola said, buckling her seat belt. "It curled my blood,"

They drove away into the fog.

…Later that night Sonny and Cher stumbled upon the castaway wig.

Their screams echoed through the night.

# Drear Window

For 40 days and 40 nights it rained that dreary Autumn, and all was gloom in Doodleburg, where Mrs. Phuddle dwelt. Hairdos fizzled, storm drains clogged, streets flooded. And everywhere a cake was baked, it fell.

Our heroine, gazing glumly out her drear window, was *this close* to building an Ark. Or, in her case, an Arkette. Mrs. Phuddle's front garden was a sodden mess of mud puddles. She'd taken to sitting for hours by this drear window, watching the rain coming relentlessly down, nursing a cold with a hot toddy.

Swimmer had the sads, his forays outdoors hurried and wet. Upon returning to the house he had to endure being scrubbed dry with a towel. At least his lady was kind enough to warm the towels first.

Fluffy snoozed the soggy hours away inside her gilded cage by the same drear window where Mrs. Phuddle huddled, watching the rain pouring down in sheets and turning Dewberry Lane into a flowing stream.

During the day Mrs. Phuddle kept somewhat busy, though she seldom left the house that rain-bespattered Autumn. She ran errands, stopped by the bakery, then headed home…to stare glumly out her drear window.

At night she watched the lights come on from her neighbors' homes, providing a small, fierce stand against impenetrable gloom. On one momentous night Mrs. Phuddle fell asleep in her chair by the window, too dispirited to slog upstairs to bed.

As the lights went out one by one beyond her drear window, Mrs. Phuddle's head nodded away and soon slumber overtook her.

A scream awoke her in the middle of the night.

She saw a light shining across the street at Mr. Advill's house.

Suddenly alert, Mrs. Phuddle focused her gaze upon the light in his living room window. His silhouette cast shadows across the wall, looming large like an ogre's from a bad dream.

*What's that he's carrying?* She wondered. It looked—gulp—*like a body bag.*

"Is that a body in that bag?" she whispered, adding, "Why on earth am I whispering?"

Chester Advill, a curmudgeonly bachelor, lived alone, as far as anyone knew. He had no pets, no hobbies outside of stamp collecting, as far as anyone knew. Once he'd owned one of those plants you supposedly can't kill due to lack of care, and it died from lack of care. He was a lonely old man.

"That's not a body in that bag," Mrs. Phuddle chided herself, still whispering. "I need to go on up to bed and stop spec—is that a knife?"

*Why was he wielding a large butcher knife at*—she glanced at the clock on the mantel—*two a.m.?*

She quickly switched off her lamp, lest he see her there, peering at him from her drear window.

But she could still see him, hacking away at something with that large saber.

"Oh, my goodness!" Mrs. Phuddle murmured, reaching for her bird-watching binoculars which she kept close at hand.

As far as Mrs. Phuddle knew, Mr. Advill was entertaining no visitors. His mother who lived in a retirement home in Florida came to see him once a year. Was she there now, unbeknownst to Mrs. Phuddle, and if so....

Her neighbor was hacking away at something, in a sort of frenzy, it seemed.

Mrs. Phuddle's throat clutched up.

What to do? What to do?

Unlike Jimmy Stewart in *Rear Window,* Mrs. Phuddle had no Grace Kelly nor Thelma Ritter to help her out.

Nor did she have a broken leg...thankfully.

*So,* she asked herself, *what would Jimmy do?*

He'd send his minions to spy on Thorwald, that's what he'd do. But Mrs. Phuddle had no minions, unless one counted a 3-inch tall wee yellow bird and a sweet brown-and-white dog as minions. Which Mrs. Phuddle most certainly did *not.*

Noticing that the rain had diminished to a drizzle, Mrs. Phuddle considered donning her raincoat and crossing the street to better ascertain the facts. While she was considering this, Mrs. Phuddle nodded off again...

A car starting up awoke her at 3:30 a.m. Peering through her drear window with sleepy eyes, Mrs. Phuddle caught a glimpse of Mr. Advill driving away.

*Where on earth could he be going at this hour of the morning?* She mused before sleep once more claimed her.

Dratted sleep.

When grey light filtered through her drear window at dawn, Mrs. Phuddle awoke with a stiff neck from sleeping all night in her chair. A glance outside showed heavy rain clouds but a lull in the downpour. Mr. Advill's old Pontiac was once again parked in his driveway.

Did she dream the events of last night? Were Mr. Advill's mysterious activities as glimpsed through sleep-hazed eyes but a figment of her imagination?

After the care and feeding of her minions, Fluffy and Swimmer, Mrs. Phuddle had settled down to a breakfast of scrambled eggs and cheese grits when there came a knock on her door.

"Who on earth is calling at this hour?" Mrs. Phuddle fussed, rising from the table.

It was Mr. Advill.

Mrs. Phuddle drew a deep breath while scanning his person for knives, guns, hatchets, and/or meat cleavers.

He appeared to be unarmed.

"Um…good morning, Chester," she managed to utter, blocking his entry. "H-how may I help you?"

Thinking, *Killer, killer.*

"Morning, Geraldine," he gruffly replied. "It's early, I know. Thing is, I need to borrow a couple of garbage bags. The big ones."

Mrs. Phuddle pursed her lips. "Garbage bags, Chester?"

He nodded. "Couldn't sleep last night. Got the notion to clean house. You wouldn't believe the junk I cleared out." He chortled. "Newspapers, *Readers' Digests,* old quilts and mattress pads."

"Mattress pads?" she echoed.

"Yup. Spent hours chopping one up to fit into garbage bags, which is why I need to borrow some."

He scowled, clearly annoyed at having to explain.

"Wait here," she told him. "I'll be right back."

She returned with two and sort of shoved them at him. "Will this be enough?" she asked, wondering if she should bolt the door.

"Thank you kindly," he said. "Noticed you were bird-watching last night. Guess you couldn't sleep either?"

"Um..er..how's your mother?"

He brightened. "Fit as a fiddle! Plays Bingo with her lady friends down there in Florida."

"She certainly lives far from you, Chester," Mrs. P opined.

"Exactly far enough," he said, turning away.

Mrs. Phuddle shut the door and leaned against it, heart thumping.

"No more sleeping by the drear window," she declared.

"Tweet," Fluffy concurred.

Three weeks later Mr. Advill's mother, one Mrs. Hagger Advill, arrived from Florida for an extended visit.

Mrs. Phuddle kept her curtains closed.

She never found out who had screamed that night.

# The Glob

"Beware of the Glob," Viola Turgid hissed into Mrs. Phuddle's pearly ear.

"What?" Mrs. Phuddle was heaping scalloped potatoes onto her plate at the First Universalist Garden of Eden Church's potluck dinner when this warning came.

"It's on the dessert table," Viola whispered before making a play for the Swedish meatballs. "Don't say I didn't warn you!"

"Beware of the Glob. Right," Mrs. Phuddle murmured, spooning Boston baked beans onto her plate next to a portion of Greek salad. *Really,* she mused, *this potluck is quite international!*

She moved down to the Kentucky fried chicken. One of the congregants had bought a bucket from the Colonel. Mrs. Phuddle was not one to sniff at fast food, not when it was crispy, delicious, and free. She took a drumstick.

Mrs. Phuddle's contribution to the feast was an apple pie, a cherry tart, and a dozen chocolate cupcakes. Make that— ahem—eleven chocolate cupcakes. (One *must* field test one's product.)

She noticed that her baked goods were placed on the dessert table next to...

"Warning," Clarissa Snortspoon muttered, sidling up to our bakeress. "You-know-who brought the you-know-what."

"The Glob?" Mrs. Phuddle glanced around. Thankfully, no one was eavesdropping.

"Remember last year, when some of us fell ill?" Clarissa continued, encroaching upon the Phuddle Personal Space. "It was her Glob!"

"Really?" Mrs. Phuddle replied. Her baby blues sought out and located the Glob's creator, Farina Flake, who was seated alone at one of the church cafeteria tables, making short work of a heaping plate of potluckedness.

"No one's touching it this year," Clarissa informed Mrs. P. "Consider yourself warned."

"Again," Mrs. Phuddle tutted, feeling as though she should duck and cover.

"Geraldine!" Viola called, waving her over to a crowded table. "I saved you a seat!"

Mrs. Phuddle joined her friend at a table crammed with members of FUGEC's choir.

"Did you get a gander at it?" Clarissa snorted. "The Glob—did you see?"

"What *could* it be made of?" Loretta Loositt added. "It looks like she just dumped a bunch of stuff from her Fridge into a Jell-O mold."

"Please, people are eating here," Viola cautioned with a sneer.

Mrs. Phuddle poked at her food, having quite lost her appetite. She was feeling a bit sorry for poor Farina Flake and her much maligned Glob.

The diners swarmed over Mrs. Phuddle's baked goods like locusts, leaving behind mere crumbs. Myra Tiddlebody's vanilla walnut fudge was also popular, as were Clarissa's store-bought chocolate chip cookies arranged on a platter to look homemade.

*Fooling no one,* Mrs. Phuddle mused.

Viola's fruitcake, recycled from last Christmas and thawed at room temperature all day, had few takers.

*Desperate people,* Mrs. Phuddle noted silently.

Then there was the lonely Glob.

Not one soul had touched it.

Mrs. Phuddle stood at the dessert table, plate in hand, contemplating the wreckage: a few cookies, a hunk of fruitcake and…

"Try it," Farina Flake urged, breathing down Mrs. Phuddle's neck.

Mrs. Phuddle sighed. *Trapped.*

She prodded the Glob with her fork.

The Glob quivered.

"It's alive!" Viola laughed.

Farina was smiling hopefully at our Mrs. Phuddle.

Visions of the ancient Christian martyrs writhed in Mrs. Phuddle's head: Joan of Arc, St. Agnes of Rome, St. John the Baptist, Thelonious Monk...

Dare she stand with them?

Mrs. Phuddle dared.

She plunged the serving spoon into the gelatinous blob.

It quivered and shook and finally yielded to the plunging spoon.

Saint Geraldine the Bakeress heaped her dessert plate with what, most assuredly, did resemble a bunch of stuff from the Fridge dumped into a mass of lime green Jell-O.

She noticed that Ms. Flake's plate was piled high with cherry tart, a chocolate cupcake, two chocolate chip cookies, and even a wedge of Viola's year-old fruitcake.

But no Glob.

"Um..." Mrs. Phuddle began, "aren't you indulging in the old family recipe yourself, Farina?"

"Nah," Farina smirked. "I got my fill of that mess growing up. But you enjoy!"

"Quite," Mrs. Phuddle replied, remaining alone at the dessert table, her plate oscillating with a quivering globule that could probably eat Chicago.

Mrs. Phuddle felt eyes upon her, heard stifled snickers at the various tables. The crowd was waiting and watching for her to eat the Glob.

"Come sit down, Gerry!" Viola hollered with unholy glee. "Eat up!"

Mrs. Phuddle pursed her lips, clutched her pearls, and stiffened her spine. She whirled about to face her tormenters, a la Joan of Arc.

*I will be brave and noble facing the unruly mob,* she told herself.

Over in a corner by herself Farina Flake had a malicious gleam in her eye, and she too was part of the unruly mob.

Mrs. Phuddle took a step forward.

Oops! She tripped on a wedge of fruitcake. The Glob hit the floor, and began to spread.

# The Bread Zone

"I see Bread People," the little hellion Tommy Landers remarked to Mrs. Phuddle one bleak November morn.

It was November First, or as some call it, The Day of the Bread.

Mrs. Phuddle fought the urge to purse her lips. Instead, she clutched her pearls. Something about Martha Flibber's young neighbor was disquieting.

"Excuse me?" Mrs. Phuddle politely responded.

She was visiting her old college roomie, Martha Flibber (of the East Coast Gibbets) for a few days. At the moment she and Tommy were alone on the back porch.

Mrs. Phuddle sat comfortably upon a cushy chaise lounge, Fluffy was in her cage near at hand, and Swimmer snoozed at his lady's feet. Martha was in the kitchen brewing up a pot of Darjeeling tea for her guest. Martha was not on the best of terms with Tommy, age nine, as he was constantly involving her in his hijinks. There was the time he tried to drown her Taddy the Tadpole in the toilet. Martha caught him holding poor Taddy by the tail over the toilet basin, an Omen-like grin on his face. Fortunately Martha rescued her wee pet, now a full-grown Toad, but still called Taddy.

Tommy pointed to a van rumbling up the hill. "Bread People," he intoned like one of the undead.

Mrs. Phuddle read the van's sign: OVEN FRESH BAKERY: Home Deliveries!

"Oh, indeed," Mrs. Phuddle replied, smiling as Martha joined them, bearing a tea tray laden with tea-time goodies.

"Oh boy!" Tommy crowed. "Baby cakes!"

He gobbled up three petit-fours before anyone could stop him.

"How are the kitties?" Mrs. Phuddle inquired, pouring amber tea into delicate cups.

Martha's seven cats lived in a state of uneasy peace with one another and the rest of the world. With both a bird—Fluffy—and a dog—Swimmer—now in temporary residence, chaos often ensued.

Add Tommy Landers to the mix and chaos seemed a time of blissful serenity in comparison.

"Tommy, does your mother know you're over here?" Martha snapped as he reached for another baby cake.

"Meh, she doesn't care," he shrugged, not knowing his mother did a little dance when he left the premises. "I was just telling Mrs. Phuddle how I see Bread People."

Both ladies refrained from rolling their eyes, which would be so unlady-like.

"Tommy, that's enough cake for you," Martha said. "You need to run along home so Mrs. Phuddle and I can talk. In private. Without you."

"Don't you wanna hear about the Bread People?" Tommy said, ignoring Martha's suggestion. He spoke again in an eerie, robotic voice. "They walk by night—pumpernickel, rye, whole-wheat. Loaves and loaves of them, with sesame seed eyes and breadstick arms and legs. You think that sourdough bread in your kitchen is just an innocent loaf waiting to be buttered, but the truth is…"

"Are you sure you're only nine?" Mrs. Phuddle said, stirring sugar into her tea.

"He's precocious, haven't you heard?" Martha scoffed. "Tommy, we've heard enough of your nonsense. Please scoot on home!"

"See that van?" Tommy continued, undaunted. "It carries the Bread People into your home. Bwa ha ha ha ha!" He threw back his tawny head and brayed.

"Oh, my," Mrs. Phuddle murmured. "Tell me, what are rolls, Tommy?"

"Please don't encourage him," Martha chided.

"Baby Bread People," he answered, scarfing down another petit-four.

"Tommy, I mean it!" Martha shrilled. "Go home!"

"Martha, shh, it's fine," Mrs. Phuddle said in her soothing manner. "Dear, I believe I hear one of the little darlings—Jassybelle, perhaps? She sounds distressed."

No more need be said. With a cry of alarm, and a flutter of hands, knocking over her tea cup, Martha rushed into the house, the door slamming behind her. From the porch one could hear a hissing, a flutter followed by hissing, a soothing murmur followed by meowing slowly devolving into contented purring.

"Tommy, come sit here beside me," Mrs. Phuddle said, mopping up Martha's spilled tea with a napkin. "You have quite an imagination. Tell me more about these Bread People. Are some of them croissants?"

He nodded. "French Bread People."

"And what do the Bread People think of our turning them into toast, or peanut and butter sandwiches?" Mrs. Phuddle's blue eyes twinkled merrily.

"I dunno—I guess they don't care," he said, yawning. He happened to be quite fond of buttered toast and PBJS. "Aren't you scared, Mrs. Phuddle? About the Bread People walking around on their breadstick legs and watching you sleep?"

"I should find that quite amusing," Mrs. Phuddle chuckled. "Sorry, Tommy, the Bread People don't frighten me."

"Me neither," the boy declared. "Say, there's one of them little cakes left. Can I have it?"

Mrs. Phuddle grinned. "If it's all right with the Cake Goblins, it's all right with me."

Tommy Landers ran screaming all the way home.

# The Beets Motel

## Or

## "Sicko"

"Goodbye, Martha, dear," Mrs. Phuddle said, hugging her old friend in farewell.

"Goodbye, Geraldine. Drive safe!" Martha cautioned. "But it's getting late. Maybe you should stay another night?"

Beyond the portal Martha Flibber-Gibbet's seven cats were yowling for their dinner. Mrs. Phuddle held Fluffy's cage in a firm embrace. Her wee yellow bird's nerves were shot, and even Swimmer seemed a bit tense.

True, she'd planned on leaving this morning, but what with one thing and another, here it was past six in the evening, and a drive of over 100 miles through dark, dense forests awaited her.

Mrs. Phuddle was not daunted.

"Don't worry, Martha. If I get tired we'll stop at a motel for the night."

Martha shook her head. "If you can find a motel that's pet-friendly." She eyed Swimmer with a dubious air.

Swimmer hung his head. "Aroo," he apologized.

"Oh, most places cater to people with pets nowadays," Mrs. Phuddle blithely replied. "We'll be fine."

It was a quarter until seven when Martha finally relinquished her friend from her doorstep. The October sun had set some time ago and it was almost dark. Twilight.

Soon Mrs. Phuddle and entourage were noodling along the dark forest roads of the Olympic Mountains, winding roads shrouded by tall cedars.

"Tweet!" Fluffy screeched as they rounded yet another sharp curve. "Tweet tweet tweet!"

"Yes," Mrs. Phuddle agreed. "One is reminded of Naomi Watts speeding through these same forest roads in *The Ring*."

"Tweeet!"

"Hurtling towards certain doom," Mrs. Phuddle continued, her icy hands gripping the wheel. "Those were nice aerial shots, though, weren't they?"

"Tweet."

"I, too, wish we'd never seen that movie," Mrs. Phuddle said. "But we did. Alas."

"Tweet?"

"No, we're not going to the spooky lighthouse, Fluffy!"

Mrs. Phuddle refused to think about *The Ring* anymore, and focused on caramel cake instead. She'd make one tomorrow, first thing.

Cake! (The Ring) Cake! Cake! Cake! (The Ring)

The road undulated past lonely cabins, the Studebaker's headlights their only guide. Mrs. Phuddle found herself growing drowsy, once jerking her head as she woke from a light doze.

"Oh, dear," she fretted. "This will never do."

"Tweet," Fluffy concurred.

Swimmer was snoring away in the back seat, twitching now and again as he dreamed of chasing squirrels. Mrs. Phuddle envied him.

"I'm far too sleepy to keep driving," Mrs. Phuddle decided. "Perhaps we should stop at an inn for the night."

"Tweet?"

"I remember seeing a sign along here on our way up."

The Studebaker wound through the dark highway another mile or two before she espied a flickering red neon sign that read "Beets Motel. \_\_ancy."

Mrs. Phuddle pulled onto the ruptured parking lot and stared at the shabby row of nine units. High on the hill above the motel loomed an ancient Victorian mansion, with one faint light glowing from an upstairs bedroom. A steep row of rickety stairs led to the massive front door.

It reminded her of something.

"Hmm," Mrs. Phuddle mused. "Perhaps we should just push on towards home."

There was a lone dark van parked outside the last unit. "Probably a serial killer staying there, resting up from his...er...work."

In the backseat both her sweeties were sleeping the sleep of the innocent. Who knew what might be sleeping in Unit 9?

Mrs. Phuddle focused her bleary gaze upon the scarecrow of a house overshadowing the motel.

"What does that remind me of? Think, Geraldine!" But she was too groggy to remember. "Sicko comes to mind...no, that's not it, either."

She yawned and stretched to clear away her mental cobwebs.

"Just another hour or so of hard driving," she muttered. " I can do it!"

About five minutes later Mrs. Phuddle swerved to avoid hitting a deer—or perhaps it was a bear? She almost hit a tree. That woke her up!

"Oh, dear!' she exclaimed, heart pounding. "This will not do!'

She turned the big car around, no easy feat on this narrow road, backing up, turning the wheel, inching forward, backing up...

In a few minutes she was back at the Beets Motel, its crimson sign flickering a warning she did not heed.

Mrs. Phuddle parked by the office. A dim light shone from within, the blinds drawn. Taking a deep breath, Mrs. Phuddle entered and approached the desk. A hand-carved wooden sign proclaimed: W. Beets, Proprietor.

A thin, middle-aged man slouched in a chair behind the desk, reading *Salem's Lot* by Stephen King. He finished reading a page and bookmarked it before glancing up at his customer. When he stood to his full height Mrs. Phuddle gulped. The man was a giant—at least six foot-nine, and rail thin. He reminded her somewhat of Ichabod Crane from *The Legend of Sleepy Hollow*.

"May I help you?" His voice was such a contrast—high and squeaky like he'd been sucking helium—that Mrs. Phuddle almost laughed out loud.

But she suppressed that urge.

"I need a room for the night, please," she said, shifting from foot to foot to stay awake. *Too much chamomile tea,* she mused.

He reached for a key hanging on the wall behind his desk, one of eight.

"Unit eight is available," he squeaked. "Just one night?"

She nodded. "Oh, yes. Just one night. And do you permit—" She held her tongue. Really, no need to mention Swimmer and Fluffy. They'd sleep, rise early, and be on their way at dawn, with no one the wiser.

He wouldn't accept her Visa card, requiring cash only. Nor did he ask for her driver's license when she signed in. Mrs. Phuddle was too sleepy to question any of this, paid with a pair of twenties, took the key and said good-night.

"Sweet dreams," the man said in his helium tones. "If you need anything, call me. I'm Beets. Wormy Beets."

Mrs. Phuddle felt a chill of foreboding.

"Beets Motel, Beets Motel," she intoned on the way to unload her car. *Why does that name sound so eerily familiar? Oh, well, it'll come to me.*

She parked in Unit 8's slot, mildly annoyed that with eight empty units, Mr. Beets had put her in a room next to the only other occupied one. She hated when restaurants did that, placing diners cheek-by-jowl at adjoining tables when the room was half empty.

She unloaded Swimmer first, leading him to a patch of weedy grass to perform his doggy ablutions. Then she took him and Fluffy into their motel room, which smelled of moth balls and mold.

"Oh, it's worse than I thought," she sighed, eyeing the sagging double bed and shabby furniture. A coffee pot with no coffee packets sat atop a rickety table next to an ancient TV set. The carpet was threadbare and suspiciously stained.

Mrs. Phuddle pursed her lips.

Really, she'd stayed at hotels in Third World countries with better accommodations. Yakkistan, for instance. (Read about Mrs. Phuddle's adventures there in *Pie, Cake, Absolve*.) She shuddered, recalling the journey she'd taken with Martha to the Burning Gates of Hell.

"Aptly named," she recalled with a lack of fondness.

She unpacked her small overnight bag and settled in for the night, brushing her teeth and washing her face with the rough cotton cloth provided. No way was she stepping into that grimy shower...

*Psycho,* she suddenly remembered. *Of course, that's what the Beets Motel reminds me of. Why couldn't I recall that before? It's almost as though...*

"Stuff and nonsense!" she declared out loud to banish that thought.

The bed creaked and sagged as Mrs. Phuddle settled into it, with Swimmer nestling at her feet. She was loath to touch the coverlet, and kicked it to the floor. She squelched the urge to search for bedbugs. Ten minutes later, she completed her search, finding none.

"Beets Motel," she murmured, eyes wide open despite her grogginess, "Beets Motel..."

"Tweet..." Fluffy replied drowsily.

"Oh, dear, I'll never get any sleep," Mrs. Phuddle moaned. "Perhaps a bit of television will settle my nerves."

She found the remote hidden under the bed and turned the set on. An infomercial about a nostril hair removal kit—CALL 800-NAS-PIKS—blared from the screen.

Mrs. Phuddle quickly switched the channel before a demonstration ensued.

A news anchor grimly informed Mrs. Phuddle of the latest doom and gloom—Roach Flu, bedbug infestations in seedy motels, mysterious murders in abandoned Victorian mansions, and the rising cost of nostril health care.

"Oh, dear," Mrs. Phuddle fretted. "This certainly won't help me sleep."

"Tweet?"

"Surely *Matlock* is showing on one of these stations," Mrs. Phuddle said. "I'd even settle for *Colombo*."

She clicked the remote again.

Naomi Watts sped through a forest road in the Olympic Peninsula on her way to certain doom.

"Oh, no!" Mrs. Phuddle gasped, almost dropping the remote in her haste. "Not *The Ring!* This can't be happening!!"

She pressed the off button and the screen went black. Mrs. Phuddle hopped out of bed and unplugged it.

She toyed with the idea of setting the TV outside or perhaps hurling a brick through the screen.

"As if that would stop her," Mrs. Phuddle said with a shudder. "She'd just keep c-c-coming."

"Tweet!" Fluffy cried.

"Y-you're right, Fluffy dear, I'm just letting my imagination spiral out of control." Still, she kept an eye on the TV screen for a few hours before sleep finally claimed her.

That's when the tapping on the wall began.

Mrs. Phuddle awoke with a rapidly beating heart.

"What in Heaven's name is that?" she quaked.

Swimmer, ever the masterful guard dog, bounded from the bed and barked.

"Shh," Mrs. Phuddle cautioned. "You're not supposed to be here."

Swimmer grew quiet, his hackles raised.

"The tapping seems to be c-c-coming from next door," Mrs. Phuddle whispered. "U-u-unit Nine."

Swimmer growled low in his throat as the rhythmic tapping continued. Mrs. Phuddle crept over to the wall and rapped back.

"Who's there?" she demanded mid-rap. "Why are you tapping on my wall?"

A ghastly moan was her only reply.

"Oh, dear," she said. "Someone in that room may be ill, or d-d-dying."

What to do? What to do?

"Tweet!" Fluffy protested, as Mrs. Phuddle began throwing on her clothes.

"I'm going to the office, Fluffy," Mrs. Phuddle said. "We'll be right back!"

"Tweeeet!" Fluffy cried, which translated from the Bird, means "Don't leave me alone in this psycho ward!"

Carrying Fluffy in her cage, and with Swimmer at her heels, Mrs. Phuddle rushed to the office. She found it locked and shuttered.

Unwillingly she raised her eyes to the house on the hill. It stood dark and silent like a waiting vulture, waiting for her...Janet Leigh...No, no, for herself, Mrs. Phuddle, to approach.

"Nope. No way. Not going up there," Mrs. Phuddle declared.

Fluffy twittered and Swimmer whined their agreement.

They went to Unit 9 and knocked.

"Hello? You in there!" Mrs. Phuddle called. "Are you all right?"

There was no reply.

She tried again, rapping loudly until her knuckles were sore, but still there was no reply. She jiggled the doorknob. Nothing.

It was locked and bolted.

Frustrated, Mrs. Phuddle returned to her own room with Fluffy fussing up a storm. She'd been quite slung around during their foray.

"Sorry, dear," Mrs. Phuddle tutted, gently setting the cage down on the table. "I'm calling 911," she said, picking up the motel's old-fashioned telephone.

But there was no dial tone. She punched in the Beets office number. Nada.

"I'll use my cell phone," she said, retrieving it from her handbag.

"Dead," she groaned. "Deader'n Marley's ghost."

At least the rapping on the wall had stopped, but did that mean...?

"We should've stayed at Martha's," Mrs. Phuddle declared.

"Tweet, tweet," Fluffy objected.

"Yes, but better the devil you know than...whatever," Mrs. Phuddle countered.

Weary and worried, Mrs. Phuddle returned to bed, but sleep was no longer a possibility. There was nothing to do but wait for the dawn, for she was still too sleepy to drive.

Just as she was finally nodding off, there was a knock on her door. Mrs. Phuddle shot up like a bullet from a gun.

"Wh-what? Who is it?" she demanded.

"Tweet!" Fluffy exclaimed.

"Grrrr," Swimmer growled.

"Open up, Mrs. Phuddle! It's Beets! Wormy Beets!"

*What kind of mother names her kid Wormy?* Mrs. Phuddle wondered as she got out of bed and donned her robe. She went to the door, but didn't open it.

"What is it, Mr. Beets?"

"Are you all right in there?" he asked through the closed door. "Mother saw you looking up at the house."

"Mother?" Mrs. Phuddle cracked the door open, leaving the safety chain secured.

"Yes," Worry squeaked. "She was watching."

"Your mother was watching us in the middle of the night?"

*Eek! Eeek! Eeek!*

Wormy slipped pale fingers through the aperture.

"She never sleeps," he explained. "Never."

"Mr. Bates...er, Beets, I'm sorry if I worried your mother, but there was someone in Unit 9 rapping on the wall for hours tonight. Then came a groaning, like someone was in pain, so I left my room to seek you out as the telephone wasn't working. Someone in Unit 9 is in trouble!"

Wormy ululated a high-pitched laugh, which sent chills through the chills already shivering up the Phuddle spine.

"But there's no one in Unit 9," Wormy squealed. "You're our only guest tonight."

Mrs. Phuddle's goosebumps flared out of control. "But I heard—and the van parked there—I don't understand!"

"Oh," Wormy said, still gripping the door frame. "The van is mine. I just leave it there for...convenience."

"I tell you, there's somebody—or some *Thing*—in that room!"

Swimmer growled, his hackles raised in warning.

"You have a dog in there!" Wormy accused. "That's against the rules, Mrs. Phuddle!"

"Rules be dashed!" Mrs. Phuddle cried, slamming the door on Wormy's fingers.

He yelled like a helium Banshee.

"Let's get the Hello Dolly out of here!" Mrs. Phuddle said to her travel companions, who seemed to be in complete agreement.

Whirling into action, Mrs. Phuddle packed them up and tiptoed to the door to peer through the peephole. There was no sign of Mr. Beets.

She dashed out to the car and quickly stowed her luggage, settled Fluffy and Swimmer in the back seat, and revved up the Studebaker.

"Homeward bound!" she declared, driving away with tires squealing.

She glanced once in the rearview mirror, catching a glimpse of a tall woman lurching down the steps from the house on the hill.

It was Mother.

She didn't look again.

# The Ladyfinger Vanishes

"One lump or two?"

"Three," Mrs. Phuddle replied as Matilda Fish proffered the sugar bowl. For the first time in their 40 years' acquaintance, the Fish Sisters were hosting Mrs. Phuddle for tea.

Usually (as in, always) Mrs. Phuddle did the honors, but this year Matilda had declared, in no uncertain terms, "It's our turn now."

Mrs. Phuddle had suppressed the reply that at 90, Matilda probably didn't have too many turns left.

"I'll make ladyfingers!" Juanita, the younger at 88, had crowed in her troll-baby voice.

Mrs. Phuddle had not failed to note the quelling glance Matilda flashed at her sister, nor her sharp rebuke.

"Nita, no!"

"Will too!"

This had gone on for several minutes until Mrs. Phuddle had stated she'd be pleased as punch to attend their tea and looked forward to Juanita's ladyfingers. She'd left them quarreling in the MacDermott's Bric-a-Brac Shoppe, and gone home to rest up for the coming ordeal.

And here she was, uncomfortably ensconced upon an overstuffed chair with hard upholstery buttons biting into her own butt...ons. Her knees were jammed up against a short round marble table with a noticeable tilt. This kept the silver tea set in a precarious position.

The room resembled an antique shop, one that was probably going out of business. One could scarcely hoist one's elbow to sip tea without knocking over a porcelain shepherdess, nor take a step without tripping over an embroidered footstool. A tasseled lamp provided a weak amber light to highlight a brass elephant, several occasional tables cluttered with figurines and doilies, a chaise lounge and matching settee. Cluttered was the only word to describe this ancient Victorian parlor.

"Delicious scones," Mrs. Phuddle commented, careful in her chewing lest she break a tooth.

The grandfather clock in the hallway chimed the hour. Bong—bong—bong—bong—bong. Five o'clock. Mrs. Phuddle sighed. One more hour to go. She longed to throw open the windows, breathe the fresh air. The parlor was overheated and stuffy, the windows shrouded in thick velvet drapes.

"Try a ladyfinger, Geraldine, if you be so bold," Matilda suggested, glancing at her sister with a sneer.

Juanita snorted around the cream puff in her mouth.

"If I be so bold?" Mrs. Phuddle queried.

"It's risky business, is what I meant."

"They're delish!" Juanita declared, reaching for another cream puff.

Mrs. Phuddle noted that neither sister had yet to touch the ladyfingers.

Mrs. Phuddle pursed her lips. She'd had issues with the Fish sisters before, once when Juanita had accidently sedated the three of them by pouring sleeping pills into the tea pot, thinking them to be saccharine tablets.

"Aren't you ladies having any?" Mrs. Phuddle hedged.

"I'm on a diet," Juanita piped, crossing her toothpick legs. She was round as a plum and showily dressed in plum taffeta with a plunging neckline, forcing one to avert one's eyes or go blind.

Matilda merely harrumphed.

"I slaved for hours in the kitchen making those ladyfingers just for you, Geraldine," Juanita whined, consuming another cream puff. "I will be so hurt if you don't eat them."

With dread Mrs. Phuddle placed one on her plate. "Don't you want one, too, Matilda? Surely you're not on a diet?"

"Why not?" Juanita squeaked. "She's fatter'n me!"

Matilda, stiffly resplendent in black taffeta, bridled with indignation. She did not, however, reach for a ladyfinger.

"Silly things, ladyfingers," Matilda finally opined, delicately sipping her tea.

"What do you mean?" Mrs. Phuddle inquired, stalling.

"Papa never allowed sweets in this house," Matilda intoned. "Absolutely forbade them! But since his departure, Juanita here has flouted his rule at every turn. Cupcakes, cream puffs, Ho-Ho's, ladyfingers!" she snorted in derision. "Papa's sanctuary is fairly swimming in sugar!"

The Plum snorted. "Papa's been dead for thirty-five years, Tildy! Time to kick up our heels!"

"Well, I for one wouldn't want to violate Papa Fish's admonitions," Mrs. Phuddle said, carefully returning her one lone ladyfinger to the platter. She had definitely noticed a weird smell...

Juanita began to whimper. "I m-made those just for you, Geraldine! I heard you say one time how much you love them! And now you w-w-won't even try one!" tears flowed into the cream puff she was chewing.

"Oh, my goodness," Mrs. Phuddle fretted. "Please, calm down, Juanita. If it's that important to you, of course I'll eat your ladyfingers!"

She paused, absorbing the image that sentence evoked, then continued, "But only if you two join me. I absolutely insist!"

Mouth set in a grim line, Matilda reached for the forbidden pastry. Juanita smiled wanly through her tears and also chose a ladyfinger.

As the three ladies were lifting ladyfingers to their lips, thunder rumbled.

Lightning flashed and crackled, as, ladyfingers poised in mid-air, they each took a bite.

The lights flickered and dimmed. The Victorian parlor was plunged into deepest gloom.

The wailing as from the bowels of a grave began.

"It's Papa," Matilda whispered, trembling as she chewed her ladyfinger. "He's unhappy."

"Oh, dear, oh dear, oh dear," Juanita whimpered.

"We broke his rule," Matilda declared.

"We're sorry, Papa," Juanita whined.

The ladyfinger stuck in Mrs. Phuddle's throat. She could not swallow. *Death by ladyfinger,* she unhappily mused.

The wind, whipped into a frenzy, rattled the shutters of the ancient mansion.

The wailing grew louder, nearer.

"Juanita, quit wailing!" Matilda snapped.

"Oooooohhh," Juanita wailed.

Mrs. Phuddle clutched her pearls. The three ladies sat in darkness, Juanita wailing, Mrs. Phuddle clutching, Matilda reciting the Lord's Prayer in Latin.

Mrs. Phuddle prayed, too, for the light to return long enough for her to make a getaway.

A thought occurred. "Matilda, didn't you say that Juanita's been violating Papa's injunction against sweets for years?" she queried. "So why is he so upset now?"

"Happens every time," Matilda replied, "but one never gets used to it."

"Totally worth it," Juanita said in mid-wail.

"Someday Papa will really let loose, Nita," Matilda warned. "Then you'll be sorry!"

The lights flickered…

Mrs. Phuddle stood to go. "Well, this has certainly been a pleasure, but I must be off—"

"The ladyfingers!" Matilda gasped. "They're gone! Oh, merciful heavens, Papa took them!"

The platter was, indeed, bereft of ladyfingers.

The wailing grew louder.

When the lamp light flickered and dimmed, Mrs. Phuddle made her escape, tripping only a few times over embroidered ottomans.

She left the Fish Sisters glaring at one another in the dark, casting aspersions on each other's loyalty to Papa.

"And, the lady vanishes," Mrs. Phuddle giggled as she slipped out the front door.

Tea with the Fish Sisters was always such an adventure.

# A Gathering of Cupcakes

Mrs. Phuddle was in a bit of a dither.

Once again she was in merry old England, visiting her cousin Lady Camilla (no, not *that* Camilla) Carlisle Barking-Buggardoff. She was awaiting a very fancy High Tea, but alas, not with the Queen. No, this day Cousin Cammy (as Mrs. Phuddle nick-named her) was hosting a High Tea in Mrs. Phuddle's honor.

The names on the guest list intimidated Mrs. Phuddle far more than the beloved Queen had. Her Highness, Mrs. P fondly recalled, had been the essence of grace once the Slapping Incident had been properly sorted out. Mrs. Phuddle didn't anticipate the same sort of *noblesse oblige* from the posh ladies coming today:

Lady Esterine Snotwell-Smythe of Upper Drippingcoast

Victoria Alexandria Catherine de Fallutin, Countess of Duncan-Donoughts

Octavia Humphund von Busch-Garten

Wilheminia, Baroness of Horssebuergar

Lady Georgiania Badrotten von Hocksworth

Then there was Mrs. Phuddle, Empress of Baked Goods

Goodness, Mrs. Phuddle fretted, didn't Cammy know any ordinary folks? People with simple, unassuming names, like

Viola Turgid? Or Clarissa Snortspoon? How about a nice, simple Martha Flibber (of the East Coast Gibbets)?

Were there no more Jane Austens or Jane Eyres left in England?

"Furthermore, what shall I wear?" Mrs. Phuddle fussed. "How does one dress for High Tea with the likes of Lady Snotdripping-Well? Or whatever her name be."

And Cammy was no help. When Mrs. Phuddle had timidly asked her cousin what she was wearing, Lady Carlisle Barking-Buggardoff airily replied, "Oh, just any old thing."

"Any old thing," Mrs. Phuddle muttered, examining the dresses she'd brought with her across the Pond.

"My lavender taffeta?" she wondered. "Perhaps too fussy?" (After all, the lavender taffeta had visited the Queen!) "One doesn't want to overdress…Any old thing? Hmmm…."

Mrs. Phuddle studied her travel ensemble, a serviceable navy blue pants suit that never wrinkled. "I look like a North Korean soldier in that," she sighed. "Perhaps with a white silk blouse and my pearls?"

She put the navy blue pants suit aside and brought out her flowery muu-muu, built for comfort. Her lying-around dress. And the flower pattern hid a multitude of sins, like spilt tea.

She shook her head in regret. "Wouldn't those fine ladies snicker if I wore that?" she put the muu-muu aside.

Then there was The Pink.

The Pink was a simple dotted Swiss cotton shirtwaist, a relic from the Doris Day Era. June Cleaver would've cleaned house in this dress, or Betty Crocker baked. Mrs. Phuddle didn't understand why the fashion industry had stopped making shirtwaist dresses. Possibly because they were too flattering, too simple?

"I should've packed another dress," Mrs. Phuddle moaned.

She reluctantly chose the North Korean Soldier, hoping only to fade into the woodwork amongst Camilla's fancy cupcakes.

"Cupcakes?" she said. "Now, why did I call them cupcakes?"

Mrs. P slapped her head. "I promised Cammy I'd bake a dozen lemon cream cupcakes for the tea! I'd better get cracking!"

She hurried down the back stairs to the kitchen, where Cammy's cook, Ida MacGillacutty, held sway. She didn't seem too pleased to have a Yank in her kitchen.

Mrs. Phuddle hastily whipped up frosting for her cupcakes in six different shades—lavender, blue, lemon, pink, orange and green.

"Silly things, cupcakes," Mrs. MacGillacutty muttered, slamming a drawer shut. "As if I weren't able to make 'em meself. Pah!"

Mrs. Phuddle quietly mixed the dough as the cook bristled nearby, banging pots and pans as she prepared scones and crumpets for the tea. Mrs. Phuddle slid her cupcakes into the oven to bake next to a tray of scones.

"Crowding me kitchen," Mrs. MacGillacutty grumbled. "Nothing will bake properly."

"Oh dear," Mrs. Phuddle said, noting the time. "I'm running late. Mrs. MacGillacutty, I hate to ask—"

"But ask you will," the cook snorted.

"I've set the timer for the cupcakes. Would you please take them out when they're done?"

"Pffft," Mrs. Mac rejoined.

Mrs. Phuddle took that as a yes.

A while later Mrs. Phuddle returned to the kitchen dressed in The Pink. She'd decided the navy blue pants suit was too utilitarian, the lavender taffeta too fussy, and the muu-muu too casual.

Thus, The Pink and pearls.

Mrs. Phuddle sniffed. "Is something burning?"

"Maybe," Mrs. Mac replied, placidly removing perfectly browned crumpets from the oven.

"My cupcakes!" Mrs. Phuddle cried, removing them from the smoking oven. Turning them onto a platter, she saw that the bottoms were burnt. "Oh, dear, they're ruined!"

Mrs. MacGillacutty hummed a happy tune as she placed her perfect scones onto a serving platter.

"Didn't you hear the timer go off, Mrs. MacGillacutty?"

"Got me hands full enough without bothering with your ruddy cupcakes, haven't I?"

Mrs. Phuddle pursed her lips. She would not be thwarted by this recalcitrant cook! "Perhaps if I just slice off the burnt bottoms, they'll be alright, especially if I slather them in frosting."

"Them swell ladies won't touch your ruddy burnt cupcakes anyhow," Mrs. Mac opined as Mrs. Phuddle desperately frosted. "Eat like tiny birds, they do. If they as much as nibble one of me scones 'twill be a shock. No, worries, lassie. But—"

Mrs. Phuddle frosted her last cupcake.

Mrs. MacGillacutty grinned, "You've smeared your pretty dress, luv."

Mrs. Phuddle examined her bodice. In her haste she'd managed to smear The Pink with cupcake frosting. And not with the pink frosting. Oh, no. 'Twas the green.

"I give up," Mrs. Phuddle said, running sticky fingers through her fluffy white hair.

Mrs. Mac laughed out loud. "And now 'tis your hair you've frosted!" she roared.

Mrs. Phuddle giggled. She couldn't help it. The cook joined her, and in a moment both ladies were holding their sides with laughter. They wheezed and gasped for breath.

"And all this bother for a bunch of ruddy swells," Mrs. Phuddle gasped.

Lady Camilla poked her well-groomed head into the kitchen. "Geraldine, what on earth? You must hurry, my dear! Our guests are arriving!"

She rushed to the parlor to do the honors.

"I'd better get changed," Mrs. Phuddle said ruefully. "I'm a mess."

"That you are, luv," Mrs. Mac agreed, with a twinkle in her eye. "Wouldn't mind sharing a cuppa with you some time."

"And we shall, Mrs. MacGillacutty," Mrs. Phuddle promised.

She headed upstairs and changed into her muu-muu. "Swells be dashed," she declared.

Comfy in the muu-muu and sandals, Mrs. Phuddle joined her cousin to meet and greet the noble ladies, who were much too grand to notice what Mrs. Phuddle was wearing. After all, she wasn't One of Them.

"Lady Victoria, allow me to introduce my American cousin, Geraldine Phuddle," Lady Camilla drawled in her upper-crust tones.

Lady Victoria, nose in air, proffered a silken hand.

"Hello, Vicky," Mrs. Phuddle grinned, deciding to lay it on thick, "pleased to meecha!"

# The Poundcake of the Baskervilles

Mrs. Phuddle adored a rich, buttery poundcake, slathered in whipped cream and garnished with fresh strawberries. Whilst visiting her English cousin, Lady Camilla (no, yada yada) Carlisle Barking etc., Mrs. Phuddle had prepared several baked delicacies for tea. A certain Lord Snottingham attended one such tea and became enraptured with Mrs. Phuddle's baked goods, especially her poundcake.

Home again in the States, Mrs. Phuddle was inundated with requests for her poundcakes from this same Lord Snottingham. He wanted her to ship him a dozen.

Mrs. Phuddle tried to deter him with, "I'm very sorry, Lord Snottingham, but the Phuddle bakery does not ship."

Lord Snottingham was not deterred. He called again and again, urging Mrs. Phuddle to make an exception in his case.

"Mrs. Phuddle," he pled in his high-toned British accent, "I beseech you to change your mind." He reached for the decanter of brandy near at hand in his study. "It's not just for me. Have you ever read any Sherlock Holmes?"

"Yesss…" Mrs. Phuddle replied, wondering where this was going.

"Then surely you've heard of Sir Charles Baskerville?"

Across the Pond Lord Snottingham sipped brandy by the amber glow of the hearth fire. A cold rain slashed the mullioned windows, but Lord Snotty (as his peers called him) was cozy as tea cups.

Not that he was drinking tea.

"Why, yes," Mrs. Phuddle admitted, watching autumn leaves falling from her maple tree. She also happened to be baking a poundcake at that very moment. "The Hound of the Baskervilles. Brilliant story."

Oddly, Mrs. Phuddle's own accent was sounding more and more British as they spoke.

"Well, it so happens that Sir Charles Baskerville is an old friend of mine," Lord Snotty drawled as his mind wandered to shared fox hunts, cricket matches and castle crawls.

Mrs. Phuddle chortled. "You're saying he's real—and still alive?" She was beginning to think Lord Snottingham had a few bats in his belfry.

"Naturally, he's the descendent of Holmes' Lord Baskerville," Snotty explained. "Charlie, as I call him. He's quite elderly, and I must say…quite ill. In fact, he may not have long to—sip sip—live."

Lord Snottingham's butler discreetly replenished the now empty brandy decanter.

Mrs. Phuddle checked her oven. The poundcake was almost done. What a lovely tea she would have today! As soon as she got rid of this pesky Lord Snotty.

"Lord Snottingham, I am very sorry to hear that," she said, not really too sorry at all, as she didn't believe his story for a minute, "however, I fail to see what this has to do with me or my poundcakes."

"I have a confession, my dear Mrs. Phuddle," he began, "but I purloined a slice of your poundcake at Lady Camilla's tea and took it to my dear, sick friend. He'd not taken nourishment in days, but he relished that poundcake of yours. Indeed, his eyes sharpened, his voice gained strength. Afterwards, he slept like the proverbial baby, or so his valet informed me…"

"How nice, " Mrs. Phuddle murmured, removing her poundcake from the oven to cool. She was becoming quite weary of Lord Snotty and his dear, sick friend.

"He's been asking for more of your poundcake ever since you left us," Lord Snotty said, watching the embers crash and burn in his stone fireplace. "I'm quite convinced it's the only thing that can save him."

"My poundcakes." Mrs. Phuddle sighed, thinking, *whipped cream and strawberries.*

She knew if she broke her rule about no shipping of her baked goods there would be no end to it. Before long Phuddle brand cakes, pies and cookies would be flying across the globe in freezer cartons. Next would come the gift catalogs, ceramic mugs, Phuddle Bobble-Head dolls, and endless cookbooks, perhaps even a stint on *Cupcake Wars.* She would require a team of lawyers to handle the ensuing lawsuits. Her simple life would be over.

Mrs. Phuddle braced herself before speaking. "My dear Lord Snottingham, I'm just not equipped for such an endeavor," she firmly avowed. "Now, if you'll please excuse me, I really need to go." And she hung up.

The next day another call from the Sceptered Isle came her way.

It was not Lord Snottingham, however.

A sepulchral voice inquired, "Mrs. Phuddle?"

A shiver ran up the Phuddle spine. That voice! That haunting sepulchral voice!

"Y-yes?" she quavered.

From thousands of miles away she heard the baying of hounds. Hounds from Hades.

"Wh-who's there?" she asked.

"Poundcake," the haunting, sepulchral voice demanded. "Send me POUNDCAKE!"

Mrs. Phuddle shuddered. This had to be Lord Basketcase!

"*POUNDCAKE!*" he thundered.

That very week Mrs. Phuddle shipped a dozen poundcakes to England, in care of Lord Snottingham, and awaited the coming storm.

# The Hills Have Pies

For the longest time the Hills had no pies. They lived lives of crabbed desolation in the mountains on the outskirts of Doodleburg, and they fed on squirrel, marmot, crow and fritters, but they ate no pies. It was a sad time.

And lo, the Hills were a close-knit, close-mouthed family who spoke little, grunted much, and played the accordion. Truly, their Celtic strains did resound and echo and yodel from Hill to Hill and from hut to hut in rain, fog, and rain.

Velveetha Cruddle was born a Hill upon the mountain, so that her name at birth was Velveetha Spam Hill, after two of the family staples. When she married Harriman Cruddle (whom the family called 'Man' for short) at 18, Velveetha moved down into the Valley, and away from the Hills. Velveetha and Man moved into Crumburg, a village known for its methane odor and scowling faces. It suited her well.

Thus, down in the Valley, amongst the Crumburgers, Mrs. Cruddle kept house and discovered the buy-in-bulk joys of KRA-Z-MART, where she stocked up on Ruffbutt Toilet Paper, prune juice, and *Charlatan Romances*. Malcontented with her life, yet still five degrees below the misery she'd felt among the Hills, Mrs. Cruddle seldom returned home for a visit.

She made her annual sojourn on April First, April Fool's Day, for no apparent reason. Mrs. Cruddle usually brought her family some kind of gift—a box of raisins, Jim Beam, tassels for Mamaw's dresses—and thus her visits were welcome, and the shotgun put away.

But the day she brought pie to the Hills—that was the day forever remembered by the Hills, and forever commemorated, as Leeching Day.

For no apparent reason.

Mrs. Cruddle had, during the course of her malcontented forays into the adjoining ville of Doodleburg, where she liked to scoff at the plethora of quaint boutiques and bistros, stumbled upon the Phuddle bakery, named *Share a Cookie,* again for no apparent reason. That day was pie baking day, and the aroma of cinnamon apples, ripe cherries, golden peaches and organic blueberries from Swooner's Farm wafted from the kitchen and into the street, like an aromatic genie.

Mrs. Cruddle, like many others that pie baking day, could not resist the allure, and wandered into the bakery as if driven by unseen forces.

Mrs. Cruddle was as puzzled by her behavior as anyone. One minute she was skulking down the sidewalk, clutching her pocketbook and scowling at passersby, the next minute she was inside the bakery, sniffing and salivating like the family dog, Smelt.

For once in her crabbed existence she could not resist a thing so pleasant. Thus it was that Veleetha Cruddle surrendered twenty of her dollars for one of the peach pies, which she took home and devoured in one sitting. She saved none for Man, as he had long since left the house for cigarettes and never been seen again.

But who cared? Mrs. Cruddle had pie. The crust was so flaky, the peaches so sweet and juicy, that Mrs. Cruddle almost despaired for what she'd been missing all these long, despairing pieless years.

Since Mrs. Cruddle rather enjoyed a strong sense of despair, this was also a good thing.

Pie, and despair.

For no apparent reason.

The very next day! Mrs. Cruddle returned to the oddly named bakery and purchased not one, but two pies, it being "Two-Pies-for-One Day." Mrs. Cruddle was also not one to pass up a bargain.

Since this day also happened to be April First, the day for Mrs. Cruddle's annual trip home, and since she was feeling not only full of pie but rather benevolent, she decided to take pie to the Hills. She carefully wrapped a cherry pie inside a plastic KRA-Z-MART bag, hopped into her 1959 Lincoln, and roared to the Hills.

"What's that thang?" Joke Boy, Velveetha's third cousin twice removed, inquired nastily as she set the pie down upon the pine trestle table.

"Looks like a big fat fritter!" Mamaw Hill proclaimed, poking it.

A bit of cherry juice leaked out.

"It's bleeding!" Mamaw screeched.

"Kill it!" Brother Junior yelled, reaching for his hickory stick.

"Is it marmot pudding?" Uncle Toad the Lesser wondered, glancing at his shotgun. "Could still be alive!"

"It's pie," Velveetha said, pulling a knife from the wall.

She cut six messy slices and plopped them onto the paper plates she'd so thoughtfully provided, along with plastic sporks. Nothing was too good for her family.

"Come on, it ain't so bad," Mrs. Cruddle urged, as her kinfolk backed away from the table as though expecting an angry alien marmot to burst from the crust and attack them.

"Here, watch me," Mrs. Cruddle said. She scooped up a bite of cherry pie with her spork and chewed, her eyes rolling with delight and despair.

"She's having a fit!" Caspar Hill, her ex-brother yelled.

Uncle Toad the Bigger grabbed his shotgun, Mamaw her broom, and Lillibit, who was either a cousin or a sister, two sporks. She crossed them to ward off evil, and perhaps marmot vampires.

"No, no," Velveetha gurgled, swallowing pie. "Really, it ain't so bad!"

"Ain't so bad" was the term of highest praise amongst the Hills.

Joke Boy grabbed up a piece of pie, sans plate or spork, and gobbled it down, face first, cherry pie juice dribbling down his beard.

"Hot diggity!" he hooted, spewing pie.

"Ain't so bad," the Hills agreed.

Mrs. Cruddle's thin lips curled into an almost smile. Her kin were filled with the same joyful despair she'd felt when first sampling a Phuddle pie.

Uncle Toad the Bigger hitched up his overalls, his pronouncement move. "From this day forth," he intoned, "every April First will be known henceforth and forthwith as Leeching Day."

He nodded solemnly for emphasis.

The Hills licked their remaining fingers.

"Leeching Day! Leeching Day!" they chanted.

"See ya'll next year!" Mrs. Cruddle hollered as she left the Hills behind, still savoring, still despairing.

"See ya on Leeching Day!" Mamaw screeched from the front porch. "Don't come without pie!"

"Lotsa pie!" Caspar yelled.

And from that day forward it was known that the Hills had pies.

For no apparent reason.

# Nightmare Kitchen

Mrs. Phuddle's niece Florry Pip was in hysterics when she called.

"Aunt Gerry, I need heeeeelp!" Florry sobbed in greeting.

Mrs. Phuddle braced herself. Florry was a newlywed, and IMPO, too young to be a wife. Her frequent hysterical phone calls were proof of that, again, in Mrs. Phuddle's opinion.

"Florry, my dear, you simply must draw a breath," she said as calmly as possible. Mrs. P settled herself in her favorite chair for the ensuing melodrama.

"My ignorant stove—hic—gasp—burns EVERYTHING I-I-I try to—hic—cook!" Florry screeched.

Mrs. Phuddle wished she dare put her phone on speaker, but that would set her dog Swimmer to howling.

"Oh, dear," Mrs. Phuddle tutted, idly thumbing through a recent issue of *Even Better Homes and Much Nicer Gardens*. "Whatever do you mean, dear?"

"It's—hic—gasp—POSSESSED!" Florry hissed. "I swear, I need an exorcist to—hic—fix the darn thing!"

"No need to swear, Florry dear," Mrs. Phuddle replied, studying a photo spread of a pale pink livingroom with lime green touches. *So soothing,* she mused. "Take a deep breath and tell me what happened."

"Last night—deep breath—I was preparing a fancy dinner for Chucky's boss, Mrs. Armenhammer. A ch-cheese soufflé."

Mrs. Phuddle turned the page. *Ah, some gentle exercises for the gardener. I really should try these.* "A soufflé, Florry? Why try such a complicated dish? Perhaps you could've made something easy, like—"She paused, thinking *Kraft Mac and cheese*—"a lovely pasta salad?

Florry pouted. "I wanted to—hic—impress her!"

"And did you?"

"The ignorant stove burnt my soufflé! It came out flat as a Frisbee and the color of toast. Burnt. Toast."

Mrs. Phuddle sighed. "Well, let that be a lesson to you," she said. "Don't ever try a recipe for company that you've never before attempted."

"I f-followed the recipe EXACTLY!" Florry shrieked.

Mrs. Phuddle held the phone away from her ear. From her birdcage Fluffy arched what could've been an eyebrow, while even Swimmer raised his sleepy head.

"Oh, then it must've been the stove," Mrs. Phuddle said, marking a recipe in her magazine for mushroom strudel.

"What I said!" Florry agreed. "Aunt Gerry, my kitchen is a NIGHTMARE!"

"The whole kitchen? Not just the stove?" Mrs. Phuddle decided the strudel recipe was too rich for her blood. She turned the page.

"Yep. The refrigerator burps and gurgles at night like a burglar tromping down the hallway," Florry said with an audible shudder. "It keeps me and Pips awake."

"Pips?"

"My dog. Chucky could sleep through a tornado, I swe— swaneee. But that dratted refrigerator is ALIVE. I tell you, it eats our food."

"That is troubling." Mrs. Phuddle thought she might have a word with her brother Belvedere about his daughter's weird notions. But, of course, that would probably upset Scarlett, Florry's mother. Best leave it be.

Mrs. Phuddle found a recipe for mixed berry cobbler on page 98. Yum, did that look good!

"You put some leftovers in there, expecting to serve them for next night's dinner and—poof!—they disappear the next morning." Florry hissed into the phone, "I think it's *hungry.*"

Then, OTOH, perhaps it wouldn't hurt for Scarlett to hear of this. "Um, Florry, my dear, have you confided any of this to your mother?"

"Are you kidding? Mama can't cook! Poor Daddy either has a sandwich for dinner, or they go out. They go out a LOT."

"Still," Mrs. Phuddle said carefully, "she's closer to you than I am. She could at least give you moral support."

"Oh, she'd just tell me to fix Chucky a baloney sandwich," Fluffy scoffed, airily dismissing her mother. "I was just hoping you'd have some advice."

Florry sounded a bit snappish.

Mrs. Phuddle put her magazine aside and drew up her courage. "Start small, Florry," she advised. "Get a basic cookbook. Learn how to prepare one dish and make it your specialty. Then, in a year or so, try another dish. Don't start with elaborate recipes like soufflés." She paused. "That's all I can tell you. It's what I did."

"But it's not ME!" Florry wailed. "It's my NIGHTMARE KITCHEN!"

"Very well," Mrs. Phuddle said. "Then you better call an exorcist."

# Fry Day, the 13th

Every Friday night Mrs. Phuddle's church, the First Universalist Garden of Eden Church, held a themed potluck dinner. These were always well attended, and the congregation enjoyed adhering to the theme, be it Greek, Italian, Moroccan, Swedish, Spanish, even Scottish (though 14 kinds of haggis was not a happy prospect). One Friday the theme was macaroni and cheese. The kids had loved that (never to be repeated) dinner.

Through the years FUGEC had sampled recipes from dozens of cultures, mostly with pleasing results, for the ladies and gentlemen of the church loved to eat and were pretty good cooks, too, in the main. Oh, there were perhaps one or two dishes it was wise to avoid if prepared by certain persons. Farina Flake's Glob comes to mind. One might dab a smidgen of the suspect dish onto one's plate, to be polite, then stir it around without actually ingesting. It was a tricky business.

The Fry Day the 13$^{th}$ potluck was a day that would live, not only in infamy, but in indigestion. It came about due to the bad luck of running out of themes.

"How about a Hawaiian luau?" Loretta Loosit suggested at the church meeting to plan the next potluck.

"We've done that one. Twice," Viola Turgid countered.

"Thrice," Clarissa Snortspoon amended.

"We seem to be running out of new ideas," Myra Tiddlebody, the pastor's wife, opined. "Can anyone think of a cuisine we haven't explored?"

There was an awkward pause, then Farina Flake's scrawny arm shot into the air. "I know!" she squealed. "Fry Day!"

"Yes, of course, the potluck is on Friday, as usual," Mrs. Tiddlebody agreed with a tiny pucker between her brows. "Any ideas—anyone?"

She studiously ignored Farina Flake, who was hopping up and down in her chair with both arms waving.

"No! I mean, let's do fried foods!" Farina cried excitedly. "You know, fried chicken, fried okra, fried ham, fried Twinkies, fried potatoes, fried oysters, fried Vienna sausages…"

There was an audible gasp from the congregation.

A gasp of fried horror.

"Fried Lipitor?" Mrs. Phuddle joked. "We'd need it."

Though they laughed at her remark, no one had another idea. Perhaps they were still stunned by Farina's suggestion.

With a sigh, Mrs. Tiddlebody said, "Very well, this Friday's potluck will be Fry Day."

"The thirteenth!" Farina gurgled. "I can't wait."

The congregation shuddered in unison, not unlike a giant bowl of lime green Jell-O.

\*

"Hmm…interesting," Mrs. Phuddle murmured to her friend Viola as they surveyed the banquet table that Fry Day, Friday the 13$^{th}$.

"It's just as Farina envisioned," Viola replied. "Fried chicken, fried ham, fried potatoes, fried oysters, fried Twinkies, and—"

"Fried Vienna sausage casserole," Mrs. Phuddle said with a grimace. "Wonder who brought that?"

They exchanged knowing glances.

Smack dab in the middle of the table, taking pride of place, was Farina Flake's creation, born of nightmare: canned Vienna sausages, a staple in any Doomsday Prepper's basement, breaded and fried til crispy, topping a gloppy mixture of lima beans, cream of mushroom soup, and cornflakes. A few random sliced black olives were scattered here and there for good measure.

"Oh, mercy," Mrs. Phuddle intoned, "this dish is a travesty of comingled canned goods."

"Shh! Here she comes!" Viola hissed.

The two friends froze.

Farina approached them with a cheerful grin, her own plate heaped with fried chicken, fried ham, etc., with seemingly no space left—alas—for her own fried Vienna sausage casserole.

"I see you're admiring my dish," Farina said, greasy fingers gripping her plate. "Well, dig in, girls, before it disappears!" With a cackle of pure evil she headed for a table.

"Disappears—there's a thought," Mrs. Phuddle murmured.

Chester Advill, an infrequent visitor to the church, excepting potluck dinners, approached with his mother, Hagger Advill, who was spending a few tortured weeks with her son.

Hagger's beady eyes fairly glistened at the sight of Farina's abomination.

"Stand aside, ladies," she commanded, "and let a body through."

Mrs. Phuddle and Ms. Turgid willingly stood aside, watching.

Hagger Advill began piling her own plate high with the Vienna sausage casserole.

"Gimme your plate," she ordered Chester.

"Mother dearest, I'd really rather not—" he wimpily replied.

"Give Mother your plate, son," Hagger commanded with steely resolve.

Chester whimpered as she piled the mess on his plate, two ladles worth.

"Eat it, son," Mrs. Advill advised. "Mother knows best."

Mrs. Phuddle had to avert her eyes as Chester followed his mother to a table, his head hanging low, like Tom Dooley's.

She dabbed a bit of fried ham and fried zucchini on her plate and joined Viola and her choir member friends at their table.

"Fry Day is a sad day," Mrs. Phuddle commented.

"Poor old Chester," Viola agreed.

"Mother knows best," Mrs. Phuddle mimicked. No one laughed. It was too sad, with Chester seated nearby, forced to consume Farina Flake's awful creation.

There was never another Fry Day potluck dinner held at FUGEC.

But dozens of Hawaiian luaus.

# The Black Cat Cake

Whenever Halloween rolled around, Mrs. Phuddle began to watch out for black cats lest they cross her path, avoided walking under ladders, knocked on wood, and practiced safe mirror handling. Seven years of bad luck was nothing to sneeze at! *Gesundheit*!

Thus it was with trepidation she listened to Cathy's voicemail message the week before Halloween.

"Hi, Mrs. P! It's me, Cathy! You'll never guess what Regina Highknocker just ordered for Halloween. Thirteen black cat cakes!"

"Oh, dear," Mrs. Phuddle murmured, ending the message. Thirteen black cat cakes sounded like bad luck every which way.

"I've already started the first black cat cake," Cathy said when Mrs. Phuddle joined her at the bakery.

Mrs. Phuddle tutted. "My dear, we'll never be able to create 13 specialty cakes in seven days, not with all our other baking requirements. And where's Izzy?"

She hastily donned her apron and began working on a batch of chocolate chip cookies.

"He's running late," Cathy explained, pouring batter into three cake pans. "Mrs. P, Mrs. Highknocker's paying us $75 per cake, how could I say no?"

"But--!"

"And she invited us to the party! She said I could bring Zack, too." Cathy smiled as she mentioned her boyfriend's name.

Izzy hobbled into the kitchen an hour later, as bruised as an over-ripe banana. His jeans were scuffed at the knees and his T-shirt smeared with grime.

Mrs. Phuddle arched a fluffy white eyebrow. "Izzy, what on earth happened to you?"

Izzy grimaced. "Ran into some bad luck on the way here," he said, tying on his apron.

His red hair stood out in tuffs, with strands of pink and green here and there as decorative touches.

Both Mrs. Phuddle and Cathy paused in mixing the dough.

"How so, Iz?" Concern shone from her lovely brown eyes.

"I was riding my bike to work, as usual," he said, setting some mixing bowls on the counter, "and rode it under a ladder on the sidewalk—"

"Oh, no!" Mrs. Phuddle gasped.

"—where they was washing windows at Gatley's Wine and Spirits, y'know?"

The two ladies nodded.

Izzy waved his skinny arms for emphasis. "Then, out of nowhere, comes this black cat crossing my path—"

Mrs. Phuddle clutched her pearls, while Cathy clutched her amulet.

"A black cat?" They whispered in unison.

Izzy continued, "Well, I hit my brakes so hard and fast I flew off my bicycle! Right over the handlebars!"

He gently stroked his bruised arm. "Skinned my elbow real good." He showed them his elbow.

Mrs. Phuddle tsked. "It's a wonder you didn't break your neck," she said. "I'll put some ointment on your scrapes."

"That's not all," Izzy said with a proud air.

Mrs. Phuddle halted.

"My feet broke a mirror, too. A great big one!"

"Oh, my goodness!"

"I remember that mirror," Cathy said, remembering. "Sidewalk sale at Flick's Fine Antiques, right next to Gatley's. They had a lovely antique mirror on display next to a wooden hobby horse."

"Dumb idea," Izzy declared. "Putting a mirror on the sidewalk."

"They obviously weren't counting on you," Mrs. Phuddle replied, looking through her purse for antibiotic cream.

Cathy chuckled. "Izzy, you've invited all kinds of bad luck today. Ladder, black cat, broken mirror, the unholy trinity of superstition."

"Nah, it's all good," he grinned, pulling out a chain from his jeans pocket. "Got my lucky charm with me."

Mrs. Phuddle smiled at his metal four-leaf clover. "That should do it," she said. "Now, let's get busy. We've got 13 black cat cakes to bake!"

But at this Izzy balked. "Thirteen?" he asked. "Ain't that an unlucky number?"

"We'll bake 14, and keep one," Mrs. Phuddle decided. "Besides, we have your lucky charm to protect us."

"How're we gonna make cat tails?" Izzy wondered.

"Maybe these can be Manx cats," Mrs. Phuddle suggested. "Tailess."

"Meow," Cathy purred, and began mixing the dough.

# Crepe Show

Mrs. Phuddle was at home, minding her own business, when she received the call.

"Hello, Mrs. Phiddle?" said Felicia Flick, one of Mrs. Phuddle's least favorite people.

"I have some exciting news!" Ms. Flick gushed.

*You're moving to Outer Freakopia?* Mrs. Phuddle thought, but did not say.

"You may have heard about Doodleburg's new local TV station, KDOOD?"

When Mrs. Phuddle only muttered a reply, Ms. Flick continued undeterred. "Well, I'm directing, and hosting, a morning talk show for the station, and we're featuring a 6 and ½ minute cooking segment."

"How nice," Mrs. Phuddle replied, surfing through the TV channels until she found KDOOD. At the moment they were scrolling through a list of local events with soft jazz playing in the background. Mrs. Phuddle found herself nodding off…

But Felicia was still babbling. "Anyway, the very first cooking segment is this Friday, and I immediately thought of you!"

"Oh, indeed?" Mrs. Phuddle said. "Why?"

"Why?" Felicia laughed. "You happen to be the best known cook in our area, Mrs. Phaddle! Don't you know that?"

"I bake," Mrs. Phuddle retorted. "I'm not a chef."

"Please say you'll do it," Felicia urged as Mrs. Phuddle frantically went through her list of plausible excuses to opt out. Just saying no never occurred to her.

"Er...this Friday, did you say?" Mrs. Phuddle stalled.

"Yes, this Friday," Felicia almost snapped. Time was money in TV Land.

"Very well," Mrs. Phuddle reluctantly relented. "I'll do it."

Immediately regretting it.

*Perhaps this will be good publicity for my bakery,* she reasoned.

"Great!" Felicia said, checking off her list. "Be here at six Friday morning for makeup. We go live at seven, with your part coming at exactly 7:39."

"My...TV is so...timely," Mrs. Phuddle noted.

"True that," Felicia said. "So please be prompt! By the way, we're highlighting France this week, so you'll be preparing crepes. You know how to make crepes, I assume?"

Mrs. P had never made a crepe in her life, but she wasn't going to admit that to Felicia Flake. *How hard can it be?* she asked herself. *A crepe is just a skinny cake. I can do it!*

"Of course," she said. "Easy-peasy."

Today was Wednesday. That gave her plenty of time to learn how to make crepes!

But first things first.

She took a nap.

And after the nap Mrs. Phuddle ran errands. And did good deeds, walked the dog, chatted with Fluffy, and baked cookies.

"Tweet?" Fluffy queried As Mrs. Phuddle explained about the TV show.

"Oh, I've got plenty of time to prepare, Fluffy," Mrs. Phuddle scoffed. "Tomorrow I will dedicate myself to the art of crepery. Is that right? Crepery?"

"Tweet tweet."

"Don't worry, my cookbooks have crepe recipes galore! I don't know why I've never made them before. I've eaten crepes, of course. Does that count?"

"Tweet."

"I confess, I'm feeling a bit giddy about the prospect of appearing on television!" Mrs. Phuddle felt a thrill of anticipation. "This is my chance to attain my 6 and ½ minutes of fame!"

"Tweet tweet."

"Oh, I don't know," Mrs. Phuddle said. "Do you think I should buy a new outfit?"

"Tweet."

Thursday morning Mrs. Phuddle went shopping for a new outfit to wear for the cooking show. She spent a few storm-tossed hours in department stores searching for the perfect TV dress—a simple but elegant frock that wouldn't wrinkle. As it happened, there was no such dress to be found anywhere. Stylish, flattering dresses with full skirts and belted waists were gone with the wind.

Alas.

She finally settled upon a blue rayon pantsuit that at least had the quality of not wrinkling nor requiring the dreaded pantyhose. Besides, she needed a new pantsuit.

Home at last, Mrs. Phuddle took Swimmer for a walk, gave him a rawhide to gnaw on, freshened Fluffy's birdseed, and had lunch.

She still had not addressed the crepe.

But the shopping expedition had so wearied our heroine she was forced to take a wee nap.

Three hours later she awoke. Groggy from her nap she made a pot of Earl Grey Tea. So refreshing!

"Goodness!" she said, sipping her tea. "I need to get cracking on those crepes!"

She got out a couple of her older cookbooks, scouring them for crepe recipes. Crepes Suzettes were featured in *The Encyclopedia of Cookery,* a regift from her old friend Molligard Hinkleburr. However, that recipe was far too complicated and time consuming for a 6 and ½ minute segment. Although she was certain she could easily master it!

There was a much simpler recipe in one of her many, many Betsy Cracker cookbooks, so she chose a simple one with a filling of whipped cream, bananas and strawberries.

Sounded yummy!

Mrs. Phuddle spent the next hour or so practicing the art of crepe making. She only ruined two or three (perhaps four) out of a dozen attempts. But the filling was not only simple, it was delicious!

*Win, win,* she thought.

Mrs. Phuddle fell asleep early that night, thinking *Makeup at six. My, my, that sounded so showbiz! Should've watched Felicia's show at least once before...*

Sleep overtook her. She dreamed of dancing crepes tumbling out of a chef's hat, tumbling and spilling and flooding the room.

*

"Good morning, Doodleburgers!" Felicia Flick, resplendent in red, gushed at 7 a.m. Friday morning. "Welcome to *Hey, Dood,* KDOOD's happy news show! Where the focus is on the pos—i—tive!"

Beaming into the camera, she continued, "Our guests today are one Alfonso Kricket, Doodleburg's newest city council member; Lotta Begooda, our local psychic who promises to demonstrate her ESP prowess; and Geraldine Phiddle, our town's preeminent bakeress, who will show us how to make the perfect crepe."

Mrs. Phuddle pursed her lips.

The first item on the agenda was "the Dood news of the day."

Mrs. Phuddle's stomach began to growl, as she regretted not getting up early enough to eat breakfast. And the plastic chair she was sitting on was so hard. She shifted uncomfortably in her seat, stomach gurgling.

Ms. Flick interviewed the councilman first. He spoke in such a boring undertone his words were hard to catch. Mrs. Phuddle let her mind drift to her upcoming crepe demonstration. She noted the small portable kitchen to one side of the set.

Once the councilman quit droning Felicia went directly to Lotta Begooda. The psychic spoke for a few minutes, explaining that in no way did she claim to predict the future.

"I give insights from what I pick up in the nether," Lotta said. She was a tall, thin woman with a mane of auburn tresses that cascaded down her back. She wore a long denim skirt with a flouncy peasant blouse and an assortment of beads and amulets, so that she clinked and clanked like wind chimes when she moved.

"We'd be delighted with a demo," Ms. Flick said, her lipstick a bit smeared.

Mrs. Phuddle suppressed the urge to point that out.

Nodding solemnly, Lotta took Felicia's hand. Gripping it firmly, and with eyes closed, Ms. Begooda began to gently sway. There was a light tinkling of beads.

"I see a galaxy of stars swirling in your aura," Lotta intoned. "And a carousel! Spinning round and round. You're riding a silver pony, and eating a kumquat. Now the galaxy of stars sweep you up and carry you off with them, where you shine like a supernova!"

Felicia preened at this analysis of her aura. "Well," she simpered, "I believe I know what this portends, but perhaps I'd best keep that to myself." She giggled in an unseemly manner, IMPO. "Thank you so much, Ms. Begooda. We'll be sure to book you again on our show. Mr. Kricket, would you care to have a reading?"

The good councilman turned red, hemmed and hawed. "Oh, thank you, no. I'd better not. I'm afraid I don't—" But he stopped right there, before declaring himself a nonbeliever. He might lose the psychic community vote when he ran for mayor. "Perhaps another time," he demurred.

"Very well. Mrs. Phaddle?" Felicia arched an eyebrow as if to dare her to say no.

"Why, certainly." Mrs. Phuddle offered her hand. She'd quite forgotten about crepes.

Lotta Begooda grasped the Phuddle hand. Once again she closed her eyes, gently swaying and tinkling.

"I see a boat, floating aimlessly down a misty river. A shadow looms over the boat, and above that a huge question mark made of fishing hooks. Something has been lost, perhaps forever..."

Mrs. Phuddle shivered. She wished to withdraw her hand.

"But," Lotta continued in her spooky psychic voice, "around the bend in this river is a meadow. Flowers bloom there, as do…cupcakes? The feeling here is sunshine, happiness and sweetness, Mrs. Phuddle."

Lotta opened her eyes, and Mrs. Phuddle noted they were a deep blue, like a vast, still lake.

"Oh, my," Mrs. Phuddle quivered. She cleared her throat. "Th-thank you, Ms. Begooda."

Felicia followed this segment with an announcement of upcoming events, while the portable kitchen was being maneuvered center stage for Mrs. Phuddle's crepe lesson.

Mrs. Phuddle remained so shaken by the psychic's reading that she was scarcely aware of events happening around her. It was like she was inside a huge wind tunnel. The next thing she knew Felicia was handing her an apron emblazoned with "KDOOD KOOK" on the bodice. Mrs. Phuddle automatically tied it around her waist.

Gazing into the camera, she said, "I've only made crepes once before in my life, but where there's a will, there's a way."

And she smiled into the river.

# The Bling

Mrs. Phuddle stared at the tiny package in her hand. She'd found it in her mailbox, not postmarked. Someone had walked or driven—perhaps bicycled—by and left it for her to discover.

She hefted its weight, hummingbird light.

There was no address written on the brown wrapping paper, just these words:

*To Geraldine*
*From your Secret Admirer*

Secret admirer? Mrs. Phuddle recalled getting a letter from her so-called "secret admirer" when she'd written a "what would Mrs. Phuddle do" column for the now defunct *Doodleburg Times.* (It had been replaced by text message updates. Not quite the same, really.)

She'd never heard from him again. Surely her S.A. was a he? Or perhaps some female fan, fond of the Phuddle baked goods, had penned that letter?

With Swimmer prancing merrily by her side, Mrs. Phuddle went inside with her mail and the mystery package.

Putting the mail aside, Mrs. Phuddle tore open the wrapping, ripping a fingernail in the process.

"Drat!" she exclaimed, toddling to the loo for a Band-Aid. The nail had torn beneath the quick, and was bleeding.

"Yuk!" Mrs. Phuddle fussed. She applied antibacterial cream and a Xena Warrior Princess bandage.

"Tweet?" Fluffy queried, tilting her wee head.

"Oh, it's nothing, dear," Mrs. Phuddle assured. "And I agree, a cup of tea would be just the thing right now."

She put on the kettle.

While the water was heating, Mrs. Phuddle carefully undid the rest of the wrapping. Inside was a squat square box. A ring box.

Opening it, Mrs. Phuddle found a milky opal ring with tiny garnets glittering from its shanks.

"Oh, my!" Mrs. Phuddle oohed.

"Tweet tweet!"

"Yes, it's quite the bling," Mrs. Phuddle concurred.

Swimmer was not so impressed. He grrred at it, deep in his throat.

Mrs. Phuddle patted him on the head, removing a small sticky note folded inside the box.

Before Mrs. Phuddle could read it, her kettle began to scream for her immediate attention.

Mrs. Phuddle bustled into the kitchen, hurriedly slipping the ring onto her finger as she made her way to the shrieking tea kettle.

In her haste Mrs. Phuddle forgot to use an oven mitt and scorched her hand on the handle.

"Ouch!" she cried, dropping the kettle onto the stove. Hot water splashed her arm. "Shoot shoot shoot!"

She poured hot water into her waiting tea pot, then ran cold water over her hand and arm.

"Ah, that's better," she sighed, as a frightened Fluffy twittered about the Phuddle head.

Swimmer barked and whined at whatever had injured his lady.

"It's fine, my dears," Mrs. Phuddle told them. "These things happen."

Returning to the mystery package as her tea steeped, Mrs. Phuddle unfolded the note and read:

*Beware!*
*Whosoever wears this ring*
*Seven days bad luck will bring.*
*Bwa ha ha*
*Yours truly,*
*Secret Admirer*

Mrs. Phuddle wrenched the opal from her finger and threw it against the wall, where it clattered and fell.

"Some secret admirer!" she declared. "Who is this vile person?"

"Tweet tweet," Fluffy cooed.

"I've already had bad luck since opening that dratted thing," Mrs. Phuddle fretted.

Her phone rang.

But no one spoke.

*

On the other end of the line Velveetha Cruddle smirked. She could tell by the stress in Mrs. Phuddle's voice that the curse of the opal ring was doing its work.

Mrs. Cruddle opened a bag of pork rinds and drank a quart of Dr. Pooper, her reward for taking that Pollyanna down a notch.

She, too, had read that "Secret Admirer" letter written to Geraldine Phuddle via the newspaper. Then and there she'd decided to rain on the Phuddle parade.

Meanwhile, Mrs. Phuddle tossed the ring, the note, and the wrapping into the trash. She sipped her tea and fretted. Seven days of bad luck were a daunting prospect.

But, aside from the torn fingernail and scalded hand (which hurt plenty), no further ill luck befell Mrs. Phuddle in the ensuing days. She had cakes to bake, tea to sip, and songs to sing.

The Curse of the Bling held no power over her.

The curse rebounded on Mrs. Cruddle. During those seven days she stubbed her toe, broke a tooth, lost her car keys, ate a rotten peanut, watched *Gigli,* and forgot to pay her utility bill.

And when her lights went out, Mrs. Cruddle had no one to blame but herself.

# The Tell-Tale Tart

*Why,* Mrs. Phuddle idly wondered, *have I allowed Lulu Sprockett to once again talk me into attending a meeting of the Doodleburg Ladies Literary Society?*

She certainly had not enjoyed her first session with the DOLLS cooing over some silly romance novel, and the chairperson, Felicia Flick, had been most condescending to Mrs. Phuddle for not having read their beloved *Man in Tan* series.

But here she was again, sitting side-by-side with the very silly Lulu, Doodleburg's local playwright and part-time pagan. Once again, to her chagrin, Mrs. Phuddle had allowed Lulu to persuade her to attend an event that flew in the face of all things Phuddle.

"Why am I so wishy-washy?" Mrs. Phuddle muttered as the DOLLS gabbed and gobbled before the meeting began. "Am I channeling my inner Charlie Brown?"

Lulu squeezed her hand. "Shh, you'll see," she whispered conspiratorially. "I've got a surprise!'

Mrs. Phuddle pursed her lips. She was not overly fond of Lulu Sprockett's "surprises."

Felicia Flick, resplendent in a grey silk suit, her platinum grey tresses stylishly shellacked, called the meeting to order with a rap of her gavel.

"DOLLS, DOLLS," she admonished with a superior air. "Let's settle down and put away the Little Chubby Cupcakes."

A minute or two elapsed as the ladies completed their calls, primped their hair, chewed and swallowed.

Once she had their undivided attention, Ms. Flick smiled her icy smile. "Today we have a special treat. Our own local celebrity writer, Ms. Lulu Sprockett, has something for us. Go ahead, Lulu."

Lulu blushed as she reached into her capacious tote bag and pulled out a book, a thin tome with a glossy illustrated cover.

"I've written a novel," Lulu announced, holding it up for the DOLLS to see. "My first romance—*The Tell-Tale Tart.*"

"Bravo!" Felicia exuded. "Pass it around for the DOLLS to examine while you tell us all about it."

"Delighted," Lulu gushed. She passed the book to Mrs. Phuddle and began to speak. "*The Tell-Tale Tart* is about a princess who—"

Mrs. Phuddle perused the cover. Tasteful, by most romance standards, she mused. A bejeweled, tiara-ed young woman gazed lovingly at the handsome profile of a steely-eyed man ensconced within a sort of cloud above her head.

"—and she disguises herself as a servant girl to save his—"

Mrs. Phuddle admired the title page with its fancy script, and Lulu's name in bold print.

She turned to page one, paragraph one.

*Lady Jeraldina, Princess of Phuddledonia, felt her lonely heart aching. Last night she had seen him again—a mere glimpse, or merely a memory? She dared not inquire his name, lest her fiancé, the cold-hearted Duke of Pearl should hear of it. That would be disastrous, not only for herself, but for her family, who needed this marriage in order to survive the onslaught of their pagan enemies. Jeraldina shuddered, remembering the feel of the Duke's cold lips on hers...*

Mrs. Phuddle passed the book to the next DOLL.

"—but I won't reveal the identity of the tell-tale tart herself, or it would ruin—"

The DOLLS oohed and aahed over Lulu's creation as they passed it from hand to manicured hand.

Meanwhile, Lulu continued, "—and I'll be signing my book at Hearts-a-Fire, Sunday from two until five. I hope you'll all be there!"

"No freebies for us DOLLS?" one of the ladies inquired.

"Umm...they're only $5 a copy," Lulu demurred.

There was a long silence.

"I'd like to pre-order a copy right now," Mrs. Phuddle declared before her brain caught up with her mouth. "In fact, Lulu, put me down for 12 copies. They'll make lovely gifts for my friends. (*Along with a large box of chocolates,* she silently amended.)

A few of the DOLLS twittered. There was a snicker or two. But Lulu didn't notice. She was beaming at Mrs. Phuddle.

"Why, thank you, Gerry!" she exclaimed, her slightly protuberant eyes luminous. "With DOLLS like you, I just know my book will be a huge success!"

Mrs. Phuddle smiled wanly. She doubted that Lulu's book would sell much more than the Phuddle Dozen.

*The Tell-Tale Tart* made it back to Lulu Sprockett, who clutched her masterpiece with bony fingers, awaiting commentary.

"Any other business?" Felicia queried the DOLLS.

"What're we reading next?"

Ms. Flick glanced at her notes. "The next hot new thing in romance literature is pop music stars. Lydia Ledbottom's latest, *Sweet Savage Twerking*, shall be our November selection. Any questions?"

In the ensuing silence, Princess Geraldine rose quickly from the table, pausing to press Lulu's knobby shoulder.

Lulu sat like a stone statue, holding her book.

"I'll be there Sunday," Mrs. Phuddle promised. "And I'll bring a friend." *Viola might go,* she mused, *if a lunch were provided.*

Lulu only nodded.

Her gaze was far, far away—perhaps upon a cloud wherein her true love awaited...

# Night of the Living Bread

Izzy bopped into Mrs. Phuddle's bakery bearing a bunch of bananas. Blackened, vastly over-ripe bananas.

"Found these behind Kroger's," he boasted. "They was gonna throw 'em away!"

"Those are from the Dumpster?" Cathy Winsome, *Share a Cookie's* manager, asked with a sniff.

"Rescued from the Dumpster!" Izzy declared, toting his find into the kitchen. "Morning, Mrs. Phuddle!"

Mrs. Phuddle glanced up from mixing the dough. "Izzy, what on earth?"

"Forty bananas, Mrs. P!" He plunked his rotting treasure onto the counter. "We can whip up a batch of banana bread."

He grinned wisely, exposing a gap in his back teeth. He'd just had a wisdom tooth pulled.

Mrs. Phuddle glanced at the clock. It was five in the morning. "My dear Mr. McLarkey, the three of us have six cakes, five pies and four dozen cookies to bake before we open at ten. I hardly think we'll have time—"

"Let's call Lola in," Izzy suggested, his brow crinkling.

"Lola's in Montana," Cathy said. "On vacation, remember?"

Regarding his crestfallen expression, and wishing to encourage initiative, Mrs. Phuddle relented. "Cathy, you and I will do the regular baking. Izzy, the banana bread is your baby. Let's get cracking!"

The bakery kitchen became a blur of flour, nuts, mashed bananas, dough, sugar, butter, eggs and chocolate chips.

Cakes popped in and out of ovens. Pies cooled on counters. Meringues rose fluffily. Cookies baked and some burned.

"There's a problem," Izzy muttered. He gripped an industrial-sized bowl filled with banana nut bread batter.

"Problem?" Mrs. Phuddle was busily whipping up a batch of chocolate chip cookies. She was dusted in flour with globs of dough sticking to her apron, her arms, her cheeks.

"Problem?" Cathy echoed as she trotted back and forth to set up the shop's counters with fresh baked goods.

Izzy gulped. "I messed up," he said, his voice breaking.

"Messed up?" Mrs. Phuddle queried as she slid a tray of cookie dough into an oven.

"Messed up?" Cathy repeated.

"Umm...I...well, you see..."

Cathy flounced into the kitchen, hands on hips. "Izzy, whatever it is, spit it out! Or do we play 20 questions all day?" She glanced meaningfully at her watch.

"We don't have enough bread pans," he murmured. "We only have two. I'm sorry." Izzy hung his head.

"Then you'll just have to bake two at a time, my dear," Mrs. Phuddle said, patting him on the shoulder. "It will be fine. Don't worry."

Izzy nodded. "Ok, Mrs. P. Thanks for the tip." And he dumped batter into two pans.

While those were baking Izzy swept the floors, cleaned the counters, and washed bowls, spoons and pans. He made himself useful.

He checked on the baking banana nut bread.

"Uh oh," he gulped.

"Uh oh?" Mrs. Phuddle frowned.

"Now what?" Cathy quizzed, again glancing at her pretty new watch, a birthday gift from her boyfriend, Zack. "It's nine, Izzy. Almost opening time."

"I know." He jerked his two banana nut bread pans from the oven. They'd swollen grotesquely, overflowing and scorching the rack.

"Izzy! What made them swell up so?" Mrs. Phuddle asked.

The odor of scorched banana nut bread wafted through the bakery.

"Izzy, did you add yeast?" Cathy scolded.

Izzy nodded. "It's bread, ain't it?"

"Did you even use a recipe?" Cathy said, examining the mess.

"Nope. I thought I knew—"

"Dear, one doesn't add yeast to banana nut bread," Mrs. Phuddle tutted.

Izzy was on the verge of tears. His grand idea had failed miserably.

"There, there," Mrs. Phuddle said, giving the boy a quick hug. "Just throw it all out and clean up the kitchen. This is really no big deal, to use Mafioso slang."

Cathy patted his head. "It's ok, cuz. Next time you find a bunch of rotten bananas, just leave them be."

The next morning, before dawn, Izzy rolled in a wheelbarrow filled with rotting apples.

"Look what I found!" he crowed. "They was gonna throw these away!"

Mrs. Phuddle and Cathy Winsome blocked his path, arms akimbo.

"Rotting apples, Izzy?" Mrs. Phuddle chided.

"Out!" Cathy demanded. "We don't serve our customers rotten fruit."

"I was thinking fried pies," he persisted. "My Mama makes 'em using old apples, and they're awesome."

Mrs. Phuddle was about to ask Izzy if perhaps he should've kept his wisdom teeth when she noticed the glitter on Cathy's left hand.

"And what is this?" Mrs. Phuddle said, cradling her manager's ring finger, where a small diamond glinted proudly.

Cathy blushed. "We're engaged," she said shyly. "Last night Zack asked me to marry him."

And in the ensuing excitement the Night of the Living Bread was forgotten.

As was the baking.

There was only enough time left to whip up a batch of fried apple pies.

They were the special of the day, and they were awesome.

# The Shuddering Jell-O Mold

Mrs. Phuddle and her brother Belvedere, "B.B." Butterflut, were enjoying a companionable post-Thanksgiving flute of sherry. Well, B.B. was drinking root beer, but he poured it into his sherry flute in tiny increments just to be companionable. They were talking over old times.

"Remember the year we had Thanksgiving at Aunt Biskit's?" B.B. chortled companionably, taking a delicate sip of his root beer.

Mrs. Phuddle twittered. "Oh, my yes. And her shuddering Jell-O mold."

Belvedere guffawed and slapped his knee. A bit of root beer splattered the sofa, but no matter. The sofa was a worn brown corduroy that disguised all manner of spills, from gravy to sassafras tea.

"I hadn't thought of that in years!" he exclaimed, spilling more root beer. "You know that Jell-O mold haunted my dreams? I was sure Daddy would find out—whew!"

Mrs. Phuddle chortled. Really, this sherry was quite strong, probably 5% proof! It was going right to her head.

"Poor Aunt Biskit," she tutted. "She had no idea the horror that green blob held for us."

"Yep." Belvedere nodded. "I always felt some guilt about that."

"And well you should," Mrs. Phuddle said with a twinkle in her eye.

"At least you managed to let your portion fall to the floor!" B.B. said, reaching for the bowl of chips by his elbow.

"No, it didn't fall, B.B.," Mrs. Phuddle replied. "It slithered..."

"Three worms," Belvedere recalled, somewhat fondly. "That's how many I managed to sneak into Aunt Biskit's Jell-O mold while it was setting."

Mrs. Phuddle shuddered. "Yes, and they were well camouflaged by the fruit cocktail."

"Unless you knew they were there." Belvedere munched chips. He really wished there was some onion dip left. But there wasn't.

"Daddy ate part of one," Mrs. Phuddle recalled. "He never noticed."

"Aunt Bisket's green Jell-O mold was sort of a pity eat, anyway," Belvedere said, crunching loudly.

"A what? A pity eat?"

He chuckled. "You know, we all had a portion so Aunt Biskit's feelings wouldn't be hurt."

"I was so shocked when I saw you slipping those poor worms in there," Mrs. Phuddle said, reaching for the sherry decanter. This trip down Memory Lane called for another round.

"But you didn't tell," Belvedere said. "Thanks for that, by the way. You saved my hide."

"I was only waiting for the appropriate moment," Mrs. Phuddle assured him. "To blackmail you."

"Blackmail! Why, Sis, that's mean!"

"I'm still holding it over your head," Mrs. Phuddle warned. "Still waiting for the right moment."

"So, Daddy ate part of one, and Aunt Biskit got two." Belvedere calculated. "Who ate the other half of Daddy's worm?"

"Please never repeat that sentence again," Mrs. Phuddle said.

An awkward silence ensued.

"It was an odd twist of fate that two of the worms ended up in her portion," Mrs. Phuddle finally added.

"Remember she said how 'chewy' the fruit cocktail was?"

Mrs. Phuddle quivered from head to toe. "Always."

Belvedere clinked his flute of root beer against Mrs. Phuddle's flute of sherry.
"To Aunt Biskit," he said.

"May she rest in peace," Mrs. Phuddle intoned. "And may she forgive us…"

# The Fudge

Mrs. Phuddle was visiting a sick friend, Matilda Fish, when she first caught a glimpse of The Fudge. It has haunted her dreams ever since, sometimes even popping up from beneath her bed like a ghoul.

Matilda, pushing 90 from the far end, was suffering from the flu.

"I told her and told her to get a flu shot," Matilda's sister, Juanita, piped up from the hallway, far away from infection. She was nibbling on a delectable square of buttery chocolate.

Matilda raised her aged head from her sweaty pillow. "What—wheeze—are you eating, Nita? Hack-hack."

She plopped against the pillow, exhausted.

"Shh," Mrs. Phuddle cautioned her sick friend. "You must rest, Matilda."

"I can rest in my—wheeze—grave!" Matilda gasped. "Nita, what—hack-hack-hack—are you—wheeze—"

"The Fudge," Juanita taunted. She scurried away from the room of sickness and imminent demise.

"The Fudge?" Matilda croaked. "That's my—gasp—secret stash! Tell her—wheeze—to give it back!"

"Let me make you a nice pot of tea and some chicken soup," Mrs. Phuddle said soothingly.

But Matilda was not soothed. "Give me my—hack-hack-wheeze—fudge!"

Mrs. Phuddle shook her head in weary defeat. When would the Fish Sisters end their lifelong sibling rivalry and make peace? Time was marching on without a truce between them.

She slipped away and down the stairs to the kitchen, passing by the parlor on her way. There was Juanita, "only in my 80s" as she often boasted, sprawled upon the red velvet chaise lounge, devouring a trashy bodice ripper and The Fudge.

Mrs. Phuddle shook her head in disgust. "Juanita, why are you so bent on upsetting poor sick Matilda?"

Juanita's brows beetled above her beady eyes. "Go away," she muttered, covering the box of candy with a copy of *Sweet Savage Shades of Mauve*.

Mrs. Phuddle jerked the book away.

"Uh huh," she grimly intoned. "Matilda's secret stash."

Mrs. Phuddle, quite against her will, found herself salivating for a piece or three of The Fudge. Her gaze locked onto black walnut fudge, peanut butter fudge, pecan fudge, caramel fudge, dark chocolate fudge, and vanilla fudge—two layers of a box that had held twenty-four. She counted 13 left.

"You—" Mrs. Phuddle swallowed, hungry now for The Fudge, "—must save the rest for Tildy, for when she gets well."

"She might not get well," Juanita countered, gobbling another piece. Twelve left.

"There, then, that's enough." Mrs. Phuddle reached for the box.

Juanita slapped her hand away. "No!" she squealed. "The Fudge is mine now!"

"Very well," Mrs. Phuddle replied, her focus fixed upon The Fudge, "what about a compromise? Save six for Matilda, and six for—others."

"Don't wanna," Juanita pouted. She clutched the fudge to her bosom.

Mrs. Phuddle was ashamed at how her voice quavered with longing. "That's selfish, Juanita. You must share The Fudge."

Juanita ignored Mrs. Phuddle, stuffing her chipmunk cheeks with The Fudge and returning to her torrid romance novel.

"Perhaps I can buy another box, then," Mrs. Phuddle suggested, wiping away a bit of drool. "If you'd just tell me where you got it—"

"Can't," Juanita grunted, turning a steamy page. "Don't know. Ask—chomp-chomp—Tildy."

Mrs. Phuddle struggled once again up the narrow twisting staircase. She paused for breath on the first landing. Only one thought drove her now—The Fudge.

She must have it.

Matilda was sleeping fitfully. Mrs. Phuddle was loath to awaken her.

But The Fudge was calling her name, and she must heed.

She must heed.

"Tildy?" Mrs. Phuddle gently shook the sick old lady awake. "Er…can you tell me…um…where you bought the…er…fudge?"

She was quite ashamed of herself.

"Nita's eating it," Matilda moaned, rolling her sweaty head back and forth in despair. "Drat her!"

"Shh, it's all right," Mrs. Phuddle cooed. "Just tell me where you procured..er…bought it."

"Craft fair," Matilda rasped. "At a booth. That's all—wheeze—I know."

"Oh dear," Mrs. Phuddle said. "You can't recall whose booth?"

Matilda snored lightly in reply.

Mrs. Phuddle hobbled back downstairs and headed directly to the parlor, where she found Juanita also deep in slumber, her spectacles askew, romance novel on the floor, and the almost empty fudge box rising and falling on her chest with each puff of breath.

Mrs. Phuddle used all her powers of stealth and cunning to reach for The Fudge. Casting aside the better angels of her nature, she gobbled down a piece of buttery pecan fudge.

Oh, Nirvana! Bliss! O sweet afternoon delight!

Once the euphoria faded, Mrs. Phuddle noticed there were only two pieces left: a peanut butter and the strawberry. Mrs. Phuddle put aside the latter for poor sick what's-her-name. She ate the PB fudge with just the tiniest pinch of guilt, which made it taste all the sweeter.

Her taste buds still doing a wee jig inside her mouth, Mrs. Phuddle cast her gaze upon a small white card resting amongst the crumbs at the bottom of the box. After devouring the crumbs, she read:

Ferrel's Fine Fudge
And Bait Shop
Beer—Bait—Fudge

The card listed an address and phone number.

Mrs. Phuddle tucked the card in her apron pocket. Remembering her sick patient at last, Mrs. Phuddle prepared a tray of hot tea and a bowl of chicken soup. The piece of strawberry fudge was also on the tray.

Seeing her friend still asleep, Mrs. Phuddle left the tray on the bedside table, and slipped away for a little excursion. Firing up the Studebaker, she drove in search of Ferrel's bait shop. She didn't even need a map.

The Fudge would show her the way.

## The Cake Whisperer

The cake sat on its stand, waiting to be cut. It trembled, waiting.

The cake was chocolate, three-layered. It was a bit lopsided, a bit flat.

Mrs. Phuddle approached the cake.

"Whish, whish, whish," Mrs. Phuddle whispered.

Suddenly, the cake righted itself. Still lopsided, but proud.

And utterly delicious, rich and velvety.

People would call Mrs. Phuddle with their cake woes.

"Oh, Mrs. Phuddle," they'd wail, "I baked this cake for little Susie's birthday party, and the frosting looks awful! I followed the directions EXACTLY from that cake decorating book. You know, with candy balloons, Happy Birthday Susie, and those fancy squiggly roses...but it's a mess! Won't you please, please come help me! Her birthday party's in one hour!"

So Mrs. Phuddle would drive her 1959 Studebaker over to the scene of the disaster, greet Susie's mother, and approach the sadly misshapen cake.

"Poor thing," Mrs. Phuddle murmured, studying the mess. "Happy Birthday Susie" was an illegible scrawl of blue icing. The candy balloons were smeary globs. And the fancy roses piped on with an untutored hand were sad little lumps of goo.

"A moment alone, please," Mrs. Phuddle said to Susie's mother, who immediately obliged, leaving Mrs. Phuddle to work her magic on the sad little homemade cake.

"Whish, whish, whish," Mrs. Phuddle whispered to Susie's birthday cake, which translated means, "You were made with love. You are given in love, and you are beautiful."

Susie's mother returned to the kitchen where Mrs. Phuddle stood by the cake.

"Why, it's beautiful!" the young mother exclaimed.

Mrs. Phuddle beamed.

And Susie's birthday cake was devoured with gusto, along with ice cream, by six excited four-year-olds.

When Mrs. Phuddle was called upon to judge cakes at the county fair, she found herself in a quandary. How to judge one cake above others, to say, in effect, "this one is the most worthy," and the others inferior?

She couldn't do it.

"I'm sorry," she told the contest organizers, "I can't do it."

"But you of all people," they objected, "should know how to judge a cake contest!"

"They would all be delicious to me," she demurred.

"Please," they insisted.

"Very well," she finally relented, girding herself.

Came the judgment day and Mrs. Phuddle's heart was heavy. She, along with two other judges, examined the array of cakes so proudly displayed on the banquet table. Caramel cakes, German chocolate cakes, strawberry cakes, pineapple upside-down cakes, chocolate fudge cakes, pound cakes, angel food cakes, every manner of cake awaited the judges' decision.

Mrs. Phuddle could sense the cakes' trembling anticipation.

"Whish, whish, whish," she whispered to each one of them.

The other judges, and not a few bystanders, glanced at her oddly.

"Mrs. Phuddle?" they inquired. "Are you all right?"

"Perfectly," she replied.

One by one the judges sampled the cakes. They made notations in their iPhones. They conferred.

"I believe the blueberry glazed cake is the best," one of the judges said. "It should get first prize."

"To me there is just no question," the second judge said. "The tri-layered peppermint cream cake should win."

Mrs. Phuddle remained silent.

"Well, Mrs. Phuddle? Your thoughts?"

"Whish, whish, whish," she said.

"Umm…" The other two judges exchanged concerned glances. Clearly, Mrs. Phuddle had lost her wits.

"My dear," one of the judges gently murmured, "perhaps you should go home and lie down."

"But we still must decide the winner!" the other judge declared.

"I've got an idea," Mrs. Phuddle said. "A lottery! We'll do a drawing and decide that way."

The other judges rolled their eyes.

"I say the blueberry glazed."

"And I say the tri-layered peppermint cream."

"Whish, whish, whish," Mrs. Phuddle said, gathering up her things.

She never found out which cake won first prize, nor was she ever again asked to judge a cake contest.

Which suited Mrs. Phuddle just fine, for when it came to cakes, she loved them every one.

Even the messy, lopsided ones. Especially those.

# And other stories...

# Mrs. Phuddle's Extreme Makeover

One morning Mrs. Phuddle peered into her mirror and saw, not the fairest of them all, but a dumpy old woman with frowsy hair, wrinkles, and sagging jowls. She went to work at the bakery, *Share a Cookie,* in a gloomy frame of mind.

"I'm frowsy," she muttered, mixing the dough. "My face looks like this lump of wet flour."

Cathy Winsome glanced up from mixing her own batch of dough to regard her friend, coworker, and mentor. *True,* she thought, *Mrs. P does look a bit tired. Nothing a makeover wouldn't fix.*

"I'm coming over to see you tonight, Mrs. P," Cathy said. "We'll give you a makeover."

"Oh, I don't know…"Mrs. Phuddle demurred. "Certainly, come on over. We'll have tea and cookies." She brightened at this happy notion.

"And a makeover," Cathy insisted. "Leave it to me. You're gonna love it!"

"Well, nothing too extreme," Mrs. Phuddle hedged. "You know, I'm rather conservative in my tastes."

Cathy just smiled, and made the cookies.

At five-thirty that evening she showed up at the Phuddle door, carrying a tote bag and a bottle of wine.

"We'll let this chill," Cathy said, placing the jug of Chablis into the fridge. "Let's get started! I'm so excited!"

Mrs. Phuddle felt the Chablis wasn't the only thing that needed to chill, but she obediently sat at the kitchen table, where the light was good.

"First, an assessment," Cathy said, fluffing Mrs. Phuddle's tresses. "My, we do need a trim, don't we?"

"Cathy," Mrs. Phuddle warned, "none of this 'we' stuff."

Cathy grinned. "Sorry."

The doorbell rang. Swimmer began to howl.

Fluffy fluttered into the kitchen. "Tweet tweet tweet!" shrilled the wee yellow bird.

"Oh, no," Mrs. Phuddle groaned. "It's Petulia Goodtimes."

Cathy shook her head. "How on earth do you understand her?"

"Who says I understand her?"

"Fluffy?"

"Oh, I thought you meant Ms. Goodtimes."

*"Tweet!"* Fluffy shrieked.

"Oh, I'll do my best, dear," Mrs. Phuddle replied, heading for the front door. "But we mustn't punch."

The doorbell rang three more times as Mrs. Phuddle toddled towards it.

"Coming, coming!" Mrs. Phuddle muttered. "Keep your shirt on."

"Tweet!"

"Fluffy, shush."

Petulia Goodtimes stood on the porch holding a jumbo bottle of Merlot.

"Hi!" she said brightly. "I brought over a bottle of red to go with the bottle of white." She strode into the living room with supreme confidence in her welcome.

"Wha—how did you know?"

"Bird-watching," Petulia somewhat cryptically replied, leading the way into Mrs. Phuddle's kitchen. "Hello, Cathy! Are we having a girl partee? Mind if I join?"

The answer seemed moot.

"Tweet."

"Fluffy," Mrs. Phuddle said. "Be nice."

Affronted, Fluffy flew to her gilded cage hanging in the living room window, as if to say, "She's all yours."

Swimmer slunk beneath the kitchen table to hide, yet still be a small, sad part of it all.

"Hello, Ms. Goodtimes," Cathy primly greeted. "Not a party, exactly. I'm giving Mrs. P a makeover."

Petulia's eyes widened. "A makeover!" she gushed. "What a brilliant idea! Let me help. I'm simply fabulous with makeovers."

"Tweet, tweet," Fluffy piped from her cage.

Mrs. Phuddle stifled a giggle.

Cathy pursed her lips a la Phuddle. "Thanks, Ms. Goodtimes, but I've got this covered."

Petulia uncorked her bottle of red and found a wineglass. Glug, glug, glug went the Merlot down Petulia's throat.

"So, what're we planning to do?" Petulia said, sitting down at the table.

"Just a little touch up," Cathy said. "Perhaps a bit of eye shadow, a hair trim…"

"I don't care for eye shadow," Mrs. Phuddle said. She longed for a cup of hot tea, sweet and strong.

"Hmm…I have just the thing at home," Ms. Goodtimes declared. "I'll be right back." She smacked the table for emphasis.

They heard the door slam as she left.

"Tweet," Fluffy grumbled, leaving her cage to flutter about her lady's head.

"Such language is unbecoming, Fluffy," Mrs. Phuddle chided. "Remember your memory verses!"

"Aroo! Aroo!" Swimmer added from beneath the table.

"That goes double for you," Mrs. Phuddle said. "We will not bolt the door!"

"Let's start with a trim," Cathy was saying as her cell phone rang. She listened for a moment, then said, "All right, Mom. I'll be right there."

"What is it, dear?"

"I'm sorry, Mrs. P," Cathy said, packing up her gear. "I've got to go. Mom's got a crisis with her car, and I need to help her."

"Oh, goodness," Mrs. Phuddle tutted. "Go, go, my dear! Rescue your mother!"

"I may not make it back tonight," Cathy sighed. "But we'll try again, ok?"

Ms. Goodtimes sashayed in just as Cathy was leaving. Mrs. Phuddle stifled a groan. Fluffy and Swimmer weren't so circumspect.

"TWEET!" roared the wee yellow bird.

"FRRRR!" growled Swimmer.

Ms. Goodtimes paid them no mind. She plopped a ginormous cosmetics bag onto the table and hung a clothing bag on the door.

"Now the real makeover begins!" Petulia crowed. She unloaded an array of powders, lotions, dyes, blushes, lipsticks, scissors, brushes, pencils, liners, curlers, and other beauty paraphernalia quite foreign to all things Phuddle.

Mrs. Phuddle struggled to rise against this tide of beauty products. "My dear, thank you, but I'd rather wait for Miss Winsome to do the honors. This was her idea, after all."

"Oh, pooh!" Petulia scoffed. "I worked 15 years for BUTI-MAX cosmetics. I can make you over so beautifully you won't recognize yourself."

"But I like recognizing myself."

"What you need is a glass of wine," Petulia said, pouring Mrs. Phuddle a generous serving. "Here, drink this. It will help you relax."

Mrs. Phuddle did need something to settle her nerves. She took a wee sip.

"Oh, very well," she said, feeling it wasn't worth a fight. "I hope Miss Winsome's feelings won't be hurt." She took another wee sip.

"Oh, pooh, pooh," Petulia poohed as she began wantonly snipping the Phuddle tresses.

An hour passed as Petulia snipped, dyed, streaked, roughed, curled, powdered, outlined, perfumed and slathered her victim. She did all but Botox Mrs. Phuddle, who, for her part, was feeling a bit fuzzy as she took wee sip after wee sip, first of the red, then of the white. Her avian and canine companions remained ominously scarce and silent.

Petulia stood back to study her masterpiece. "Perhaps just a tad bit more of shading," she murmured, reaching for her blush brush.

Mrs. Phuddle drowsed through another round of makeover machinations, quite relaxed, indeed.

"Ah," Petulia said at last, "now for the crowning touch!"

"A tiara?" Mrs. Phuddle asked hopefully.

"A dress," Petulia replied. "Close your eyes."

Mrs. Phuddle sighed heavily but obliged. She so needed a nap...

"Stand," Petulia commanded.

Mrs. Phuddle stood.

"Take off your dress," Petulia said.

"This is beginning to seem like a scene from *Fifty Shades of Grey,*" Mrs. Phuddle objected. "Not that I saw the movie. Nor read the book."

Petulia sniggered.

"Just to be clear."

Mrs. Phuddle kept her eyes shut as her neighbor helped her squeeze into a skin-tight sheath. Zipping it up was torture.

"What you need," Petulia said, struggling with the zipper, "is a girdle."

"What I need," Mrs. Phuddle countered, "is a hot soak in the tub."

"Oh, no you don't! We're going out to dinner to show off the New You!"

"Mirror," Mrs. Phuddle replied tersely.

"Do you have a full-length?"

"Upstairs."

They headed up to Mrs. Phuddle's boudoir, our heroine mincing her steps in the tight Spandex, pleather, or whatever the heck it was.

She braced herself before the full-length mirror and gaped at the clown gaping back at her.

"I look like a frowsy old tart!" she groaned.

Petulia frowned.

"Waiting for last call," Mrs. Phuddle added.

"And getting no offers," she continued.

"Well, I wouldn't know about that," Ms. Goodtimes tartly replied.

Mrs. Phuddle looked like a clown, her cheeks ruddy with rouge, neon-blue eye shadow drowning her own baby blues, false eyelashes as big as spider legs and twice as scary, pouty Kardashian lips, and worst of all—pink streaked spiky hair.

And the dress! The dress! Mrs. Phuddle looked like a clown-faced green sausage, and not in a good way. She bulged in the most unseemly places.

"Undo, undo!" Mrs. Phuddle urged.

Petulia's face fell (not much, it was too tightly Botoxed). "I think you look amazing," Petulia responded.

"I am amazed," Mrs. Phuddle replied, trying to uncase herself from the dress.

She could see Petulia's sad reflection in the mirror, standing behind the clown. "My dear," Mrs. Phuddle said, attempting to turn, " I thank you for your efforts, but this look is simply not me. Now, if you don't mind, I'd really like to take that hot bath."

"Fine!" Petulia thundered, flouncing away. "Stay a frump forever for all I care!"

"I wonder how Houdini did it," Mrs. Phuddle mused, straining to free herself from her Spandex prison. She could hear her neighbor downstairs, loudly packing her cosmetics bag and slamming the door on her way out.

"Oh, dear," Mrs. Phuddle murmured, but not too contritely. She knew Ms. Goodtimes would soon recover.

She soaked in the tub for an hour, washing herself clean and shiny. She scrubbed her hair—twice—but the pink spikes remained. That would just have to grow out, a memento from her Extreme Makeover.

# Mrs. Phuddle Thinks She Can Dance

It was a sadness in Mrs. Phuddle's life that she'd never been built for ballet. Even as a little girl, she was never svelte. Rather, young Geraldine Butterflut had been a bit rotund, with short, chubby (but sturdy) legs and rosy cherub cheeks. Yet her mother, Hortense 'Horty' Butterflut, had caved in to her daughter's wishes, or as some might call it, incessant whining, and enrolled her in ballet classes.

Imagine, if you will, a peach prancing amongst the asparagus. Short, plump (but sturdy) little Geraldine of the shining blue eyes was the peach. The other little girls with their pencil thin forms and perfect postures were the asparagus.

Her plié was more of a plea.

Her tutu was too, too much.

And her glissade was more of a slide than a glide.

Gerry Butterflut's era of ballet dancing was mercifully brief, and she forlornly returned to her paper dolls.

Her ballerina paper dolls.

It was a sadness.

Mrs. Phuddle came of age during the "dirty dancing" craze, which she wisely eschewed. There was nothing "dirty" about Miss Butterflut. She was pristine. Perhaps a bit prissy, but we digress.

Instead, she turned to pies and cakes.

As in, the baking of, the sharing of, the eating of.

Also cookies.

Geraldine met Will Phuddle when she was a sophomore at the Blue Mountain College for Chaste Young Ladies, where she roomed with Martha Flibber (of the East Coast Gibbets). Though Geraldine could not dance, Will fell for her shining blue eyes and her baked goods.

Despite finding True Love with Will, cakes, pies, and cookies, Mrs. Phuddle's inner ballerina remained strong, and sang sadly to her in the wee hours of the night.

In her dreams Mrs. Phuddle was as graceful as a gazelle, her tutu a thing of shimmering light and air. She looked nothing like a peach in a tutu.

One long ago morning at breakfast, Mrs. Phuddle said to hubs, "Will, I think I can dance."

Will cocked an eyebrow. He was a warm, fuzzy teddy bear of a guy. He was peering through his gold-rimmed eye glasses at the sports section of the newspaper. Although he didn't smoke a pipe, he would've looked good doing so. Loose brown cardigans and plaid shirts suited him well. His reddish brown hair was always a bit messy. He was adorable.

"Hmm?" was his distracted response, as he was absorbed in a story about the Mariners' new third baseman who showed real promise.

"Will, I'm signing up for ballroom dancing at the Y," his wife declared. "And so are you!"

"Yes, dear," he murmured, wondering why his favorite player, Charles Brown, was being sent back to the minors. Such an injustice!

Thus a week later Will was somewhat surprised to find himself on the dance floor at the local YMCA. Together, Will and Wife attempted the salsa, the Lindy Hop, the mambo, tango and samba. Their tango got tangled; they hopped on each other's toes; their polka was quite poky. Their mambo, samba, and salsa, not to mention the cha cha and bossa nova, were a confusing mix of missteps.

Only the waltz matched their moves, even though their timing was off by a few beats. While everyone else was one-two-threeing, the Phuddles were one-two-stuttering.

But it was not a sadness.

At the Grande Ball marking the finale of their lessons, Mrs. Phuddle was radiant in blue velvet, Will resplendent in his rented tux with blue velvet cummerbund.

Stuttering together to the beautiful *Tennessee Waltz*, they both thought they could dance.

And in the arms of her one true love, Mrs. Phuddle final felt like an asparagus.

# Mrs. Phuddle, Voted Off the Island?

"Ah," Mrs. Phuddle sighed as she sank into a beach chair on the Isle of Sapri. She sipped an ice-cold Shirley Temple, prettily festooned with a tiny pink umbrella. "Sheer heaven."

"Bed bugs," Viola Turgid countered. "My bed was crawling with them."

Mrs. Phuddle pursed her lips to suppress an irritated rejoinder. Her dear friend Viola would probably complain that Heaven's streets of gold were too hard on the feet.

"I itched all night, too," Martha Flibber-Gibbet chimed in. She wore a huge floppy hat, wrap-around shades, and enough sunblock to trigger an eclipse.

*Really,* Mrs. Phuddle mused, *why didn't Martha just stay in their room with the curtains drawn?*

Mrs. Phuddle applied herself to sipping her drink and enjoying the gentle lapping of the ocean onto the shore.

"So timeless," she murmured, gazing out to sea. "And what a delicious, delicate breeze. Aren't these palm trees just divine?"

"Just don't stand beneath them," Viola groused. "I almost got beamed with a falling coconut during last night's luau. Could've killed me!"

"Did the poi taste funny to you?" Martha asked with a whine. "My tummy was queasy for hours afterwards. Between that and the itching, I scarcely got a wink of sleep."

"You were snoring plenty," Viola retorted.

Mrs. Phuddle sighed. "Really, girls, can't we try and focus on the positive?"

Their waiter from the hotel deposited fresh drinks on the table—another S.T for Mrs. Phuddle, a Mai Tai for Viola, and a mango daiquiri for Martha.

Mrs. Phuddle glanced at her watch. "Drinking before noon? Tsk, tsk."

"We're on vaycay," Viola snorted. "Anything goes."

"Especially the bedbugs," Martha added, sipping her daiquiri. "Yum. Delicious! The drink, not the bedbugs."

The three ladies made quite the picture of elderly holiday bliss—Viola in her usual attire, a flowing purple caftan and emerald green turban; Martha swathed like Lawrence of Arabia to prevent sunburn; and Mrs. Phuddle. Our fair lady sported a pink bathing suit last seen in the Sears Roebuck Catalog circa 1955, a wide-brimmed straw hat and a pair of pink Sandra Dee sunglasses. She was ready for Beach Blanket Bingo!

Their tiffs meant nothing amiss, as the three friends were like peas in a pod, daisies on a chain, links in a locket. Or so Mrs. Phuddle believed...

After precisely 15 minutes of basking on the beach the ladies went to lunch at the hotel. They sat inside to avoid further sun damage.

"Fifteen minutes is the recommended time for sun bathing, you know," Viola said for the umpteenth time that day.

"Don't want to cook like a lobster," Martha added, knocking her chair askew and shaking the table as she settled in with her paraphernalia.

Mrs. Phuddle and Ms. Turgid gripped their place settings and goblets until Martha was fully seated.

"Earthquake Martha," Viola joked.

She was met with a quelling glance from Mrs. Phuddle. "So, ladies, what's on our agenda today?" she asked after the server took their orders. "Tennis? Swimming? A hike up Mt. Tushykhominga?"

The ladies laughed with great hilarity.

"I have a new mystery by Phyllistina Bludworthy I'm eager to read,' Mrs. Phuddle said as her shrimp cocktail was placed before her. "So I plan to settle in the Tiki Garden and read the afternoon away with a pitcher of lemonade."

"A nap for me," Viola said. "We were up so late last night at that luau." She dug into her Spam musabi with gusto.

"Well, I don't care to nap with a bunch of bedbugs," Martha announced, too loudly, IMPO. "So I'm going to the spa!"

Martha flung both her arms and strands of chop suey for emphasis.

Mrs. Phuddle shuddered. "Martha, dear, please no more talk of bedbugs while we dine."

"And watch the flinging," Viola added. "There's chop suey all over the floor."

"Whatevs," Martha replied, flinging another strand of chop suey.

The threesome went their separate ways after lunch, Mrs. Phuddle to her haven by the koi pond in the Tiki Garden, Viola to their room for a nap, and Martha to the hotel spa for a mud bath, facial, and Serbian massage.

Mrs. Phuddle spent a peaceful afternoon alone in her oasis, totally enthralled with *Death by Pastry Brush*. All clues pointed to the baker, Fannie Popover, as the killer, but Mrs. Phuddle was certain of her innocence. Fannie was too obvious a suspect unless the author was pulling a reverse double twist. Besides, how could anyone who baked such delectable scones (as lovingly described in buttery detail by Ms. Bludworthy) commit such a heinous murder, and with a pastry brush at that?

Viola's afternoon wasn't as refreshing, as she battled the bedbugs.

"This is outrageous!" she grumbled, swatting them with Mrs. Phuddle's house slipper. "I'm complaining to the management!"

She hunted down the hotel manager (no easy feat), and brought her to the room.

"Voila!" Viola declared, ripping back the sheets to expose the hypothetical creepy-crawlies. (They were quite invisible.)

The manager made a great pretense of examining the sheets. "I see nothing," she stated. "Perhaps you are experiencing an allergy."

Viola crossed her scrawny arms and glared. "This is unacceptable," she said. "I will give your hotel a zero rating on Yelp."

The manager grunted. "Very well, we will fumigate this room, although it is unnecessary, as there are NO BEDBUGS in this fine hotel. Five stars."

"Fumigate?" Viola snorted. "Not good enough. We demand a new room, with fresh, CLEAN bedding."

Meanwhile, Martha was being pummeled by Djorak, the masseuse, immersed in slime, plucked for blackheads and pounded with hot rocks. She was oiled and emulsified until she emerged from the spa slicker than the wake of the Exxon Valdez.

Martha oozed her way back to their hotel room, ready for a nap. "That massage was so thorough!" she declared to the empty room. "But what is that awful smell?" Her nose twitched like Peter Cottontail's amongst the lettuce. "It reeks of chemicals in here!"

She finally noticed none of her things were in the room. None of their things were in the room!

"We've been robbed!" she screeched, running down the hall with flailing arms.

Viola, napping peacefully in their new room, was awakened by Martha's shrieks. Groggily she climbed out of her nice, cool, clean bed and opened the door.

"Martha!" she hissed. "In here! New room!"

"What's going on?" Martha wailed, flinging herself at Viola. She slid off.

"Whoa!" Viola bridled. "You just slimed me."

"Just tell me what's going on!"

"Our old room was fumigated due to bedbug infestation," Viola explained. "Now, calm down, Martha, and for Pete's sake, take a shower!"

"But how did I manage to get in?" Martha wondered, still flailing, but at a distance.

Viola shrugged. "Someone forgot to void your key, I guess. Modern hotel efficiency! Ha!"

\*

Returning to her room two hours later, having finished her mystery (the victim's husband did it by hiring a body double to establish his alibi), Mrs. Phuddle was flummoxed to find her key would not open the door.

"Well, I'm flummoxed!" Mrs. Phuddle exclaimed. She tried the key three more times. She rattled the doorknob and pounded.

"What on earth?" she muttered. She couldn't call her companions, as there was no cell phone service here in the Outer Tushy Islands.

Mrs. Phuddle pursed her lips and strode to the concierge in the lobby. "My room key doesn't work," she stated with just a hint of pique. "And I don't know where my friends are!"

The concierge, weary after a long day of fumigating rooms, sighed. "Maybe they voted you off the island," she half-heartedly joked.

Mrs. Phuddle considered the possibility. Had Viola and Martha abandoned her? Moved on to another hotel? Would they leave without saying goodbye?

"Nonsense," Mrs. Phuddle concluded. "We're like peas in a pod, daisies on a chain, links in a locket. They would never vote me off the island!"

"Ah, here we are—they changed rooms." The concierge said, consulting her registration book. "You're now in room 202. " She handed Mrs. Phuddle a new key.

But when Mrs. Phuddle entered 202, Viola and Martha were not there, either. But their luggage was.

"Two flibbergibbets," she muttered, heading to the hotel restaurant.

And there they were, in the Tiki Lounge, half hidden by gigantic frozen cocktails aswarm with umbrellas, plastic flamingos, curly straws, and whipped cream.

"Hello, ladies," Mrs. Phuddle greeted them pleasantly.

"We ordered you a frozen mango daiquiri," Martha said, pointing to a colorful drink the size of a basketball.

"Ah," Mrs. Phuddle sighed, sipping from the fruity concoction. "Thank you for not voting me off the island."

# The Ghost of Downtown Blabby

Mrs. Phuddle paused to inspect a suit of armor standing guard in one of the vasty halls of Downtown Blabby.

"So uncomfortable looking," Mrs. Phuddle murmured to her cousin Lady Camilla. "And rather short, too."

"Ahem," their tour guide, Harmonica Wyresmythe, prompted them. "If you would care to join us, ladies?"

Mrs. Phuddle and Lady Camilla obediently joined the group paused before an enormous oil portrait of a lovely young woman in Victorian dress.

"Such a sad fate," Harmonica sighed. "Downtown Blabby is legendarily haunted by the Dowager Countess, pictured here," she intoned. "Her husband, the sixteenth Earl of Blabby, died tragically young in an auto accident shortly after his wife gave birth to their son and heir." She paused to let that sink in. "It's said they roam these halls, ever searching for one another, always a mere corridor away…" She sniffled and brushed away a wanton tear. "Some say you can hear them calling each other's names…night after endless night…"

Someone in the group chuckled. Probably an American.

Mrs. Phuddle shivered in delight. She simply adored haunted houses, and a haunted castle was a thousand times better. To think that she, Geraldine Phuddle, would be sleeping in one of those haunted bedrooms tonight! She couldn't wait…

But wait she must. Mrs. Phuddle and Lady Camilla joined the other guests touring with them at dinner promptly at eight. (Eight o'clock for dinner was very late for our Phuddle, but oh so fashionable. When in Blabby, do as the Blabbers do.)
The formal dining room was huge and drafty, the furniture heavy and dark. The Earl himself presided at the head of the table to dine and converse with them. Another thrill!

The Earl was a heavy imbiber. As he drank and waxed large on his family's noble history, he began to lean to the left, almost falling out of his chair. As he leaned, Duncan Hines, the butler, would pause to realign his master with a discreet but effective nudge.

"He's like a human Tower of Pisa," Mrs. Phuddle whispered to her cousin as they tucked into their seven course dinner.

Just as she was speaking the Earl fell over with a crash, his legs tangled up in the rungs of the heavy chair, which remained stolidly upright.

"Oh, dear!" Mrs. Phuddle gasped.

The other guests gasped, as well. A few chuckled discreetly. One or two guffawed aloud.

"Most unseemly," said Mrs. Phuddle.

Only Lady Camilla remained unperturbed. "Think nothing of it," she coolly advised. "Enjoy your kidney pie."

In a snap Hines reseated the inelegant Earl.

"Yesss," the Earl drawled, tapping his goblet for more joy juice. "We were discussing my family crest, were we not?"

"We were not," Mrs. Phuddle replied.

This won her an arched eyebrow of disapproval from her cousin, while the Americans grinned. The Earl emptied his wine in one gigantic gulp. He then proceeded to hiccup. He bounced in his seat with each eruption.

"My," Mrs. Phuddle commented as the hired help cleared their table for the next course. "I never realized how classy—"

"Geraldine," Lady Camilla cautioned. "Hush."

Mrs. Phuddle giggled.

The dinner continued in this manner, with the Earl of Blabby imbibing, hiccupping, leaning and falling. It soon became routine and not worth commenting upon. After dinner Hines guided the inebriated Earl to his quarters, while the housekeeper showed the guests to their rooms.

If Mrs. Phuddle was not in awe of the Earl, she was of her room. It was gloomily grand, just as a haunted castle bedroom should be. A queen-sized four-poster bed heaped with embroidered pillows beckoned her to slumber. Scarlet and royal blue patterned rug cushioned her feet, and the heavily curtained windows shrouded one in sepulchral seclusion. Dark, heavy furniture, including a dresser, wardrobe, and wingback chair completed the ensemble.

"Ah," she sighed. "This is perfect...for a haunting."

A maid had already unpacked and put away the Phuddle luggage, and kindly laid out a nightgown. An exquisite golden box of chocolates rested on her bedside table next to a tall brass lamp.

"One could get used to this," she decided, sampling a chocolate.

Mrs. Phuddle prepared for bed, performing her ablutions in a tiny drafty half bath she shared with the bedroom next door. "Harrumph," she grumbled. "No hot water."

The bed was so high she needed a small staircase provided to climb onto it. She nestled beneath the covers with *A Connecticut Yankee in King Arthur's Court* by Mark Twain, and read for a few minutes before the power of sleep compelled her. She had to climb down from the stairs to reach the brass lamp and switch it off.

"One doesn't have Gumby arms," she complained to whatever spirits were listening. She climbed back up in pitch darkness, almost tipping over the mini-staircase. Exhausted from her exertions, Mrs. Phuddle was soon lightly snoring.

It was around two a.m. when a ghastly moaning awakened her.

"What on earth?" she said, sitting bolt upright, momentarily confused. It was so dark! Where was she?

Then she remembered…within the hallowed, haunted halls of Downtown Blabby.

But what was causing that eerie ululation?

"Woe, wooooooe, woooooe," someone or some thing was moaning as he, she—or It—shuffled down the corridor.

"Oh, my goodness!" Mrs. Phuddle fretted. She pulled the covers up to her eyes. "It's the ghost of Downtown Blabby!"

Indeed, one heard dreadful footsteps, dragging along the floor, along with the incessant, pitiable moaning.

Mrs. Phuddle was too scared to turn on the light. Besides, it was too dark to even see those dratted steps one needed to descend.

"Like climbing K2," she groused, to, hopefully, no one.

"Woooe, wooooe, wooooe...."

The thudding began.

Footsteps pounding down the hall.

A stifled cry—

A sharp bang!

Screams in the night!

"Oh, dear, oh, dear, oh, dear!" Mrs. Phuddle fretted. Was her door locked? Would that even matter if the Thing in the Hall wanted to get her? "Oh, dear, oh, dear, oh, dear!"

She heard voices in the corridor—beautiful, blessed American voices!

"What's that?"

"Are you getting video for this?"

"I'm gonna sue!"

Yes, beautiful, normal American voices.

Suddenly Duncan Hines was in charge. Mrs. Phuddle, quivering beneath the covers, heard him say, "Would everyone be so kind as to return to his or her room? The staff shall handle this…er…incident."

She heard grumbling, followed by doors slamming, bolts secured.

Finally, silence.

Mrs. Phuddle waited for an hour in the darkness before sleep claimed her once more. She slept late, arising at nine. The sun struggled in vain to penetrate the heavy bedroom drapes. Yawning, stretching, Mrs. Phuddle carefully climbed down from bed and got ready for her day. The enormous pendulum clock on the landing was striking ten by the time she found her way to the breakfast table.

Lady Camilla was already seated, fresh as an English rose, buttering a scone.

"Good morning, Geraldine," her cousin greeted. "Sleep well?"

Mrs. Phuddle detected a smirk.

"No, I did not," she retorted. "Didn't you hear all the commotion during the night? The wailing, the thudding, the dragging, banging, and screaming? It sounded like someone was being slaughtered in the corridor."

Lady Camilla sipped her tea, definitely smirking. "Quite thrilling, was it?"

"No!" Mrs. Phuddle exclaimed. "How can you sit there so calmly? I tell you, someone was *murdered* in my hallway last night! It sounded like the Earl of—"

The Earl of Blabby strolled nonchalantly into the dining room. Perfectly coiffed and immaculately attired, he was the picture of refined British nobility.

"Good morning, Lady Camilla, Mrs. Phuddle," he greeted them. "I hope you slept well?"

He, too, was smirking.

Lady Camilla and the Earl of Blabby shared a discreet chuckle.

Mrs. Phuddle sputtered, "What's going on?"

Duncan Hines and one of the servers appeared bearing fresh rashers of bacon and kidneys, placing them on the buffet table.

Mrs. Phuddle glared at them, too.

A few of the Americans trickled into breakfast, sleepily rubbing their eyes and scratching. Beautiful, blessed Americans.

"Dude, last night was a trip!" one of the young men declared, piling his plate high with bacon and eggs. (No kidneys.)

"Got our money's worth," another said.

"I'm still suing," a third replied.

Mrs. Phuddle pursed her lips. "What exactly happened last night?" she demanded.

"Performance art," Lady Camilla drolly informed her.

"We hope you enjoyed the show!" the Earl said with a smile. He remained quite upright throughout the entire meal.

# Mrs. Phuddle's Gothic Nightmare

*Why,* Mrs. Phuddle wondered, *is a hearse pulling into my driveway?*

"Oh, dear," she said, "is this an omen?"

"Tweet! Tweet!" Fluffy replied, which translated from the Bird, means "Close the curtains! Bolt the door! Batten down the hatches!"

And Swimmer, Mrs. Phuddle's brave brown-and-white dog, not being quite as articulate, barked and grred from behind Mrs. Phuddle's skirts.

Mrs. Phuddle peered through a crack in the curtains. She was most decidedly not expecting company, much less a mortician. But why else would a death car be pulling up to her house, unless…

Something rattled in Mrs. Phuddle's throat.

A death rattle?

Mrs. Phuddle gasped as her old friend, Martha Flibber (of the East Coast Gibbets) got out of the passenger side of the hearse.

"Land sake's alive!" Mrs. Phuddle exclaimed, resorting to one of her Grandma Butterflut's expressions. "What can this mean?"

Martha was lurching and flailing her arms, so that at least was normal. But who was driving this...vehicle? In answer, a tall, thin figure, garbed entirely in black, a personage with huge, ghoulish eyes, unfolded itself from the driver's side of the hearse.

Mrs. Phuddle wished she were wearing her pearls so she could clutch them.

Fluffy, firmly perched atop Mrs. Phuddle's shoulder, shrieked in birdy horror: "Tweeeeeeeet!"

Mrs. Phuddle gulped as Martha and her spectral companion approached the front door...and knocked.

Fluffy fluttered to the security of her gilded cage, but Swimmer courageously accompanied his lady to the portal...two steps behind.

"Gerry!" Martha gushed as Mrs. Phuddle ushered her two visitors inside.

"Er...hello, Martha," Mrs. Phuddle murmured, casting a furtive glance at the woman in black.

"Gerry, do you remember my cousin, Holly Goth-Lightly?" Martha asked by way of introduction.

"Helly," the woman in black corrected. "I've changed my name to Helly."

"I'm not certain I've had the pleasure," Mrs. Phuddle replied, appraising Martha's cousin with a discerning eye.

Helly Goth-Lightly was, as mentioned, tall and rail thin. Her hair, long, bushy, and unnaturally ink black (think Cher in *Moonstruck*) was streaked in shades of pink and purple. Her complexion was ghostly pale, her eyes shadowed in red and black. Chains draped one shoulder that attached to a skull bracelet rattling from one skeletal arm. A tattoo of a two-headed asp coiled up her neck to her pointy chin. What Mrs. Phuddle could see of her arms were also tatted with swirls, daggers, angels, roses, drops of blood, and…a Twinkie? Could've been a bright yellow coffin…Could've been a Twinkie. One couldn't be sure. Ms. Goth-Lightly's eyebrows were pierced several times with tiny silver rings. Her nose sported a larger one. And oh, dear Lord, her tongue was pierced with a silver stud.

Mrs. Phuddle suppressed the gagging sensation rising in her throat.

Helly had to be at least fifty, Mrs. Phuddle surmised, and was therefore perhaps just a tad too old to be going Goth. But she kept this opinion to herself.

"Won't you…er…ladies have a seat?" Mrs. Phuddle gestured towards the rose patterned settee.

"Pastels," Helly grumbled.

Mrs. Phuddle lowered herself onto the blue velvet wing chair. "To what do I owe the pleasure of this visit?" she inquired, hoping she sounded sincere.

Martha flailed an arm, nearly knocking over a vase of tulips. "Well, you see, Helly here has a problem—"

Mrs. Phuddle pursed her lips. "Helly Goth-Lightly," she said. "Quite an unusual name. A play upon Truman Capote's Holly Golightly, one presumes?"

Helly's head seemed to be bopping to some inner rhythm. "Huh?" She focused heavily mascaraed eyes upon her hostess.

Martha tittered nervously. "Her real name is Holly Flibber, of the West Coast Lightlys. Or, as we know her, Holly Flibber-Lightly.

Helly/Holly shrugged, chains a-rattle. "Yeah. I changed it to suit me." She glanced around at her surroundings. "Cool bird," she commented, espying Fluffy. "Big head."

Fluffy pretended not to hear.

So did Mrs. Phuddle.

Swimmer crouched by his lady's side, ready to do battle if necessary, or at least grrr a little bit.

"About this problem---,"Mrs. Phuddle prompted.

Martha glanced at her cousin, who appeared to be chanting. "Helly wants to de-Goth," she explained. "We thought— I thought maybe you could help?"

Mrs. Phuddle sighed. "I'm not sure I understand."

"I'm too bleeping old for this bleep anymore!" Helly suddenly wailed. "I'm 56 bleeping years old. Look at me! I'm a mess! I just wanna be normal so people don't point and laugh at me when I walk down the street!"

Helly stood up and paced, flailing her arms as she ranted. *The Flibber is strong in this one,* Mrs. Phuddle mused.

"We're doing an intervention," Martha continued, running skinny fingers through her ginger-grey hair.

"I'm afraid I have no experience in...er...de-Gothing," Mrs. Phuddle replied.

She rose from the wing chair with a determined air. "What we need is a nice cup of tea, with perhaps some cinnamon crisps," Mrs. Phuddle declared. "And then we may discuss Holly's de-Gothing."

"Got any hemp tea?" Helly asked with a snigger.

Mrs. Phuddle bridled, but momentarily, before forging ahead. "No, my dear," she answered. "I'm fresh out."

"Figures," Helly muttered. She pulled a pack of Nicky's from a skirt pocket. "Okay if I smoke?" She started to light up.

Mrs. Phuddle stopped in her tea-brewing tracks. Her lips pursed so hard they almost came out the other side.

"It most certainly is NOT okay," she retorted. "Put that flame out at once!"

Martha began to moan and flail.

"Martha, may I speak to you for a moment, please?" Mrs. Phuddle jerked her head towards the kitchen.

Swimmer and Fluffy joined them while Helly Goth-Lightly remained behind, sulking and muttering.

Mrs. Phuddle's head throbbed. She needed tea, and quickly. She put the kettle on and set out the tea things.

Then she turned to Martha, who was quivering.

"Explain," Mrs. Phuddle demanded. "In 500 words or less, please."

"I'm so sorry," Martha began. "Perhaps we should just leave."

Mrs. Phuddle softened. "Not until we've had our tea. What is Helly's story, dear?"

"Holly went Goth back in the 80s, as I understand it, just to aggravate her parents. Well, she aggravated them so much they disowned her. That just made Holly dig her heels in, so to speak. She's lived on the fringes now for thirty years—working in video stores, waitressing in bars, singing in alternative night clubs. She has quite a lovely voice, really. But like she said, Holly's 56 now, and she wants to abandon this lifestyle, but doesn't know how."

"Her attitude could use an adjustment," Mrs. Phuddle said, pouring tea. "I didn't appreciate her lighting up in my home."

"Oh, she likes to push the boundaries," Martha explained. "See how far she can go, test the waters."

Mrs. Phuddle huffed. "That's silly. I'm not her parent. And she's not fifteen."

*

After a charming repast of tea and cookies, while Martha and Mrs. Phuddle chatted amiably and Helly munched noisily through the cinnamon crisps and purposely slurped her pekoe, Mrs. P got down to biz, as they say. (But not as Mrs. Phuddle says. Mrs. Phuddle gets down to business, if you must know.)

"Holly," Mrs. P began, "I'd like to help you if I can, and if you're sincere."

"Oh, spare me the lecture," Helly scoffed.

"Very well." Mrs. Phuddle stood. "This has been so pleasant. Thank you for dropping—"

"Sorry!" Helly shrilled, waving her hands like Stevie Nicks with a tambourine. "Sorry. Sorry. It's just my reflex, y'know? Part of what I'm trying to change."

"Not trying very hard," Mrs. Phuddle replied stiffly. "I will not be made to feel a prude in my own home. Now, you will either heed my advice, or—" She nodded towards the door. "You're free to go."

Helly slumped against the settee. Martha sipped tea, trying to disappear into the rose petals.

Mrs. Phuddle sat back down. "Fine. Let's proceed. As a first step, might I suggest a nice transitional shade of purple in lieu of solid black?"

"Purple? Purple?" Helly screwed up her mouth and eyed the ceiling, tapping her pointy chin with a black fingernail. "I just don't see it…"

Mrs. Phuddle glanced at Martha with exasperation. Martha was also studying the ceiling as though Michelangelo had painted it. "I really don't know how to do this," Mrs. Phuddle finally concluded.

"Maybe a shopping trip?" Martha suggested hopefully. "Helly could try on some clothes, dip her toe in the water."

"It probably needs it," Mrs. Phuddle murmured.

Helly shrugged her indifference.

Mrs. Phuddle threw up her hands. "I'll give it an hour."

*

Three hours later, surrounded by heaps of discarded clothing, Martha, Helly and Mrs. Phuddle were still ensconced within a dressing room of N.V. Saxx. Mounds of matronly frocks, flowery sundresses, subdued purplish pantsuits, and matching sweater sets spoke volumes of frustration.

Helly examined herself—again—in the full-length mirror as Martha and Mrs. Phuddle hovered nearby. Helly was wearing a navy blue pants suit, black pumps, and a red scarf for a hint of color.

She looked most unhappy.

"I just don't see it," Helly muttered. "This look is not me."

"It's not Helly Goth-Lightly," Mrs. Phuddle kindly rejoined. "But perhaps this look suits Holly Lightly?"

"Holly Lightly, Holly Lightly," Helly echoed, shaking her head with nary a rattle. "So dull. So normal."

"How about Holly Flibber-Lightly?" Martha countered. "That's not dull."

"Not normal, either," Mrs. Phuddle whispered.

"You'll have to get your name legally changed again, I suppose," Martha mused.

Helly frowned. "But I like Helly Goth-Lightly," she whined. "It sets me apart."

Mrs. Phuddle had had enough of N.V. Saxx, clothes hangers, Martha, and Helly whatever-her-name-be.

"I suggest we adjourn to the Doodleburg Tea Shoppe for refreshment...and some serious discussion," she said.

Seated around a small table at the tea shop, Mrs. Phuddle enjoyed a bracing sip of Darjeeling. "Ah, that hits the spot," she sighed. "Any thoughts, Helly—Holly—in our attempts to de-Goth you?"

Helly shrugged, dipping a macaroon into her cup of hot black coffee. "Maybe Goth is the real me," she said.

"Oh, Helly, "Martha moaned. "Why do you have to be so contrary?"

Mrs. Phuddle held up a hand. "You know, I think Helly is right," she said. "Surely there's room in this world for varying styles of dress."

Helly grinned. "And maybe once in a while I'll even wear purple."

Mrs. Phuddle smiled. "With a red hat?"

"Hmm..." Helly screwed up her mouth again. "No, but maybe I'll adopt a red cat."

All three chuckled at that.

"Here's to Helly Goth-Lightly!" Mrs. Phuddle saluted, holding up her tea cup.

"Just call me Granny Goth," Helly replied, and slurped her coffee.

# An Evening of Literary Despair at Viola Turgid's

Four somber-visaged women sat in a semicircle facing Viola Turgid. These were four of Ms. Turgid's closest friends, those who could come up with no valid, believable excuse for not attending this first meeting of the Turgid Poetry Society. Four women who had climbed the steep, rickety steps leading up to this point of no return, Viola's three-room apartment overlooking a pharmacy.

Mrs. Phuddle was one of those helpless women sitting in the semicircle of doom, her spirits sinking. There weren't even any refreshments in evidence, just the dry, endless recital of Turgid poems.

"Now, this is a good one," Viola merrily introduced her seventh poem of the evening. Four somber faces struggled to smile, to show a token of interest...and failed.

"Ode to a Chickadee," Viola began.

"I think that I will never see—"

"Sounds familiar," Lulu Sprockett murmured. As Doodleburg's self-proclaimed Literary Laureate, she resented having to listen to Viola's drivel.

Viola cast her critic a quelling glance and began again.

"I think that I will never see
A bird so cute as a chickadee—"

"And now if I could only pee," one of the other ladies muttered. Could've been any one of them, except Mrs. Phuddle, of course. She'd never utter anything so uncouth.

"Who said that?" Viola snapped, her green turban canting a bit.

The ladies of the semicircle stared back at her with dead, innocent eyes.

"Ahem. Once again...

"I THINK THAT I WILL NEVER SEE
A bird—"

A groan of literary despair issued from the semicircle of doom, precise source unknown.

"—so cute as a chickadee
A bird that chirps and tweets all day
And in her nest an egg doth lay—"

"Speaking of which," Lulu chortled.

Viola glared.

"Laying an egg," Lulu finished.

Mrs. Phuddle glared at Lulu. "My dear, do you wish to leave these premises sometime this eon?" she turned to Viola. "Please proceed, Viola."

The semicircle sank deeper into gloom. Lulu pouted. Martha Flibber (of the East Coast Gibbets) fingered her Tibetan prayer beads. Clarissa Snortspoon was secretly sleeping, her eyes at half-mast, drooling a bit, too. She snored lightly. Only Mrs. Phuddle remained heroically stoic.

Viola prodded Clarissa with the point of her shoe. "Wake up, Clarissa!" she demanded.

"Wha?" Clarissa snorted.

"Please, Viola, continue," Mrs. Phuddle urged, praying for either an end to Viola's verse or a quick, merciful death, whichever came first. "And please start at 'and in her nest an egg shall lay.'"

"Doth," Viola amended. "In her nest an egg DOTH lay."

"Aiieeiggh," Lulu moaned.

Viola shook her papers (her many, many papers) to begin again...

"And in her nest an egg DOTH lay
What great hand and what great eye
Did teach this little bird to fly?"

"Mixing two great poems into one, are we?" Lulu sniped.

Mrs. Phuddle gripped Lulu's arm. "Lulu, hush," she cautioned.

Viola finally surrendered. She tossed her precious pages aside and hung her head in defeat, turban askew.

"I give up," she said, heartbroken.

Mrs. Phuddle and Martha rushed to her side, murmuring soothing words of solace and encouragement, straightening the turban that covered Viola's wispy hair. Lulu remained firmly in place, arms folded, mouth grim.

Clarissa was lightly snoring.

Martha began gathering up the strewn papers, managing to crumple a few and scatter others. "Oh, dear," she fussed, hurrying after sheets blown in the wind of her flailing arms. "Why are they so dratted contrary?"

Mrs. Phuddle turned her fierce gaze towards Ms. Sprockett, who remained stubbornly unrepentant.

"Lulu, you owe Viola an apology!"

"She owes me two hours of my life!" Lulu snidely rejoined. "I'm going home!" She gathered up her purse and coat and headed for the door.

"Surprise!" Petulia Goodtimes declared, entering as Lulu opened the door. "I heard from Horris about tonight's literary evening, and I brought goodies!"

She hoisted a wine bag holding two bottles and another bag fragrant with warm yeast donuts.

Never had an entrance been so timely. Corks popped, wine was poured, donuts were devoured.

Within ten minutes five mellow ladies sat in a semicircle, munching and swilling, and only inwardly cringing as they listened to "Ode to a Chickadee" from the beginning:

"I think that I will never see
A bird so cute as a chickadee—"

# A Second Evening of Literary Despair

Such a success was her first meeting of the Turgid Poetry Society, that Viola immediately convened another. The usual suspects were in reluctant attendance. Some had resorted to a few nips of strong drink beforehand. Mrs. Phuddle, indeed, even she, had braced herself with a flute of sherry before mounting the narrow wooden steps leading up to Viola's flat. (She'd been reading British mysteries again.)

As before noted, a lugubrious semicircle of women faced what Viola was now calling The Reading Chair. So far only Viola had graced it. This would soon change, as a sort of *coup d'etat* took place in due course.

Tonight each lady was fiercely clutching her own precious masterpiece, each heart yearning for Viola to end her monotonous recital so that they could assume The Reading Chair and spread their treasured words to a waiting world.

Myra Tiddlebody, the pastor's good wife, had written a book of verse, as well, a tome titled *A Gladdened Heart Made Young by Spring.*

Martha Flibber-Gibbet's offering was a children's book featuring seven cats—not her own cats, mind you. She didn't want fame to spoil them.

Lulu Sprockett, Doodleburg's preeminent playwright and creative spirit, strove in vain not to roll her eyes, yawn, or scream death threats as once again she sat listening to Viola's turgid verse. Lulu had written a brilliant play and couldn't wait to read it aloud to a captive audience.

And then there was Mrs. Phuddle, whose own literary offering was an essay titled *Why I Bake.*

Meanwhile, Viola slogged on.

"This next poem," she began, scanning her audience for signs of appreciation, "is called *Methinks.*"

Her voice strong, and showing no sign of flagging, she read:

"Methinks that Time's a standing bell
Upon which comes the deathly knell.
Methinks of—"

"Why is the bell standing?" Lulu snapped.

Viola gurgled in surprise at the interruption. "What?"

"She asked why is the bell standing?" Martha explained, waving her manuscript in the air. "A bell doesn't stand."

"It hangs," said Lulu.

"Poetic license, perhaps?" Mrs. Phuddle gently suggested, wondering if this literary evening would ever be over, what with Viola reading perhaps every single poem from her voluminous *Thoughts Upon a Tristan Shanty.* The phrase "Tristan Shanty" rang a bell—pun intended—in Mrs. Phuddle's memory. Wasn't that a poem by Wordsworth, or rather a novel by John Steinbeck? No, that wasn't it...

"May I continue?' Viola grated.

Met with a stony silence, Viola took that as an affirmation.

Clearing her throat, she began again.

"Methinks that Time's a STANDING bell
Upon which comes—"

"Tolls would be better."

"Upon which COMES the deathly knell.
Methinks of Spring at times like this—"

"My poems are about Spring, too," Myra Tiddlebody whispered.

"Many poems are," Lulu replied. "Unfortunately."

This comment triggered a gentle melee. Viola glared at the reverend's wife. The reverend's wife pursed her lips. Lulu Sprockett threw up her hands, muttering something about eternal damnation, which Mrs. Phuddle thought should've been Myra's line. Martha flailed her arms about, knocking her wig askew. (Martha was having a bad hair year. Wigs seemed to be the solution.) Mrs. Phuddle arched an eyebrow. She refrained from clutching her pearls, sensing that she would need that contingency at a later date in this literary evening.

Finally, after several minutes of pandemonium, Mrs. Phuddle stood to address the unruly semicircle.

"Perhaps we should allow Viola to complete her recitation of *Methinks* and then move on to the next—ahem—literary offering? I believe Lulu was up next?"

Viola huffed a bit about being rushed, but at last completed the reading of *Methinks*, a 74 stanza ode to joy. (It merely seemed longer.)

She plopped onto the vacated seat in the semicircle as Lulu assumed The Reading Chair.

"I will read Act I, Scene I, of my latest play," Lulu primly began. "If you wish to know the rest of it—" Her bushy eyebrows waggled a small threat—"you may purchase my work at local bookstores."

"Loco bookstores," Viola muttered.

Lulu wisely chose to ignore that comment and began her reading of *The Heartbreaker Cometh*.

Act I Scene I

(*A lady's parlor. Grey curtains. Two women dressed in black. A sense of impending doom prevails. The constant ticking of a mantel clock is the only sound, until—*
The doorbell rings!)

Chantrelle Littlebottom (*a young woman, very austere, with great dignity*)
"I'll get it."

Ramona Plantagenet (*a stern woman, hair in a bun, dressed in old-fashioned attire*)
"I wonder. Could it be--?"

(A small groan issued from the semicircle. A sense of impending doom prevailed.)

Chantrelle—"It may be." (*She clutches her heaving bosom.*)

Ramona—"He, after all these years—"

(*The doorbell rings again.*)

Chantrelle—"Dare I? Ramona, I'm so afraid."

Ramona—"But what if it's not—"

"Answer the blasted door already!" Viola thundered. (Not part of the play.)

"The suspense is killing me," Martha deadpanned. (Ditto)

"Who could it be?" Viola giggled. "Whoooo? Whoooo?"

Once again Mrs. Phuddle felt moved to address the literary group.

"Ladies, ladies," she pled. "We must respect one another's work. Please save your negative thoughts for your journals. And remember, we have pie and cake waiting at the end of our—er—session."

Indeed, our kind Mrs. Phuddle had baked both a caramel cake (her favorite, after coconut) and a lemon ice box pie for the refreshment phase of this literary evening, if and when it ended...

Lulu was allowed to continue with her play. As it turned out, Chantrelle opened the door after the third ringing of the doorbell, to greet her long-lost lover Averill Chatsworth, who'd been gamboling about the Alaskan wilderness for many years. Unfortunately, Chantrelle had lost faith in Averill's return, and had become engaged to a rising young dentist, Lloyd Oppenweider.

How this situation resolved itself would not be revealed until Act 5, Scene 15, involving numerous costume changes and two sword fights.

"Let me merely suggest," Lulu said at the close of her reading, "one will need several hankies long before the thrilling denouement."

"I need them now," Viola muttered.

With austere dignity Lulu Sprockett rose from The Reading Chair and resumed her place in the semicircle. Martha Flibber-Gibbet assumed the position.

"*Seven Cats for Seven Days,*" Martha proudly began. "Mrs. Fillibuster lived alone in a great big teapot with her seven cats—"

"Hardly alone," said Lulu.

"—Ronnie, Bonnie, Sunny, Bunny, Catnip, Cowslip, and Ben. They were cats of all description—black, white, black with white paws, white with black paws, calico, ginger, and grey. Each cat had its own day to be honored.

"Monday was Ronnie's day. On Mondays he had the run of the house while the others were cloistered in the cat room, which was full of toys and climbing structures for them to climb upon…"

Martha's story continued in this vein for several endless minutes that seemed like endless hours. By cat six some in the semicircle were audibly snoring. By cat seven the blood temperatures of the audience members had reached 95 degrees and dropping. Never had caramel cake and lemon ice box pie seemed so elusive…so enticing.

At long last Martha completed her tale of the seven cats and their seven long, uneventful, redundant days.

Mrs. Phuddle snapped out of her reverie as Myra Tiddlebody approached the chair. She had about her an air of prim efficiency, and a soupcon of pomposity.

She cleared her throat and began reading her verse.

"*A Gladdened Heart Made Young by Spring,*" she said, announcing the title…again.

"Must be winter," Lulu intoned.

Mrs. Tiddlebody was not deterred. "My first verse is titled *Heed Not the Serpent's Whisper.*"

"Heed not the serpent's whisper,
Nor bite the forbidden fruit
For the asp is but a shyster
Your soul he doth recruit.

"Nor heed his devious cunning
For his heart is black as night—"

"Black as night," Lulu scoffed. "How original."

Myra glowered at the serpent.

"For his heart is **black as night**
If to him you come running
Thou wilt—"

"I'm wilting , " Lulu giggled.

Four pairs of eyes cast quelling glances in Lulu's direction.

"Thou wilt never see the Light," Myra finished. "Really, ladies, some of us are being quite rude."

"Agreed," Mrs. Phuddle agreed. "I don't see how we can continue these literary evenings with such disharmony."

"Sorry, sorry," Lulu said, not sounding at all sorry.

Somewhat mollified, the reverend's wife continued with several more samples of her verse, whose titles are listed below for your edification:

*A thrill Most Unbecoming in a Maid*

*She Dwelt within Well-Trodden Bower*

*Ode on a Greasy Urn*

*The Ebon Heart, the Wither'd Flower*

*Ne'er Cast Your Net Upon Befoul'd Waters*

*Strange Flits of Passion She Has Known*

At the end of this hour and a half reading of poems about young ladies who had not taken the purity oath, a few in the semicircle (exactly four) were pining for the zombie apocalypse to end their suffering.

But there was still one more reading to go.

Mrs. Phuddle's.

With a thrill most unbecoming in a maid, she went to the seat of honor. *"Why I Bake,"* she read. "Because it's good."

She closed her manuscript. "Now, who's for pie and cake?"

There were no refusals.

# Mrs. Phuddle Strikes a Match

To her horror, Mrs. Phuddle found herself out on a date. With a man. A very strange man. This was all Viola Turgid's fault, for convincing her to join a one-month trial offer as a member of Lockinglips.com.

"Locking Lips?" Mrs. Phuddle had protested. "Sounds most unseemly."

But Viola had been adamant. At age 59, she was beginning to fear she'd be a life-long spinster. Since Horris Winterspeare, the handsome choir director of FUGEC, was already taken (drat that Petulia Goodtimes!), there were no eligible men left at the church from which to choose.

Single men, yes.

Eligible men, no.

Make of that what you will.

Thus Viola had boldly gone where no FUGEC choir member had gone before, and signed up for the month-long trial membership in Lockinglips.com. And convinced her best friend into doing the same.

"But, Viola, I don't want to date," Mrs. Phuddle had argued in vain.

"Oh, pshaw!" Viola had counter-argued. "You can't pine forever for Will, Geraldine! He wouldn't want you to."

"Would too."

"Wouldn't."

"Would."

"Wouldn't."

This went on for a few more minutes until Viola made the final argument. "Face it, Geraldine. Will is not coming back. He's gone forever, and it's time for you to get back in the game!"

"This is no game," Mrs. Phuddle rejoined.

But finally Viola's incessant whining wore her down, and just to get some peace and quiet, Mrs. Phuddle agreed to enroll in this unseemly sounding dating site.

Online, whatever that meant.

With Viola watching over her shoulder, Mrs. Phuddle entered her profile:

Age: Old enough to know better.
Sex: No
Occupation: Baking cookies
Personality: I always liked Elvis, but Paul McCartney was my dream man. He really was "the cute Beatle!"
Marital status: Yes

"Oh, Gerry, you'll never attract any men with that lame profile!" Viola sputtered. "Let me jazz it up for you." She began editing the Phuddle profile.

"I loathe jazz," Mrs. Phuddle replied. "Can I put that in?

Mrs. Phuddle slapped Viola's busy typing hands. "Quit that!" she cried, deleting "Looking for some action."

"I am NOT looking for some action! Let me see your profile, Missy!"

She read, with Lockinglips a-pursed:

Age: 'Twix Twelve and Plenty
Sex: Very much a female
Occupation: File clerk for County Court
Interests: Singing, dancing, travel, fine dining, red roses, diamonds, splendor in the grass, fun fun fun! I'm a fun girl!
Personality: Tons of it!
Marital Status: Still searching for Mr. All Right

Mrs. Phuddle blushed. "Why, Viola, 'splendor in the grass'? I'm ashamed for you!"

"That was a great movie!"

"But very suggestive, no? What would Rev. Tiddlebody say?"

"He won't know, unless he's a member, too," Viola replied. "Now, let's just sit back and wait for results to come pouring in."

Three days later Viola received two responses, and made two dates for coffee.

Mrs. Phuddle's lone response came a week later and she reluctantly made a date for lunch with a certain Mr. Arnold Chuckinblaster.

His profile read:

Age: 67
Sex: M
Occupation: Taking care of Mother
Interests: Finding a good, sturdy woman with strong lifting arms. Must not flinch at bedpans. The patience of a saint is a plus, too.
Personality: I enjoy reading aloud to a receptive audience the works of Edward George Bulwer-Lytton, a highly underrated author, who, in my humble estimation (for it is my estimation that matters here, hence and forthwith), stands head and shoulders above such popularly acclaimed writers such as Charles Dickens, who, though prolific, indeed, also, too, had the undeniable bent of a left-wing socialist and rabble-rouser, whilst Mr. Bulwer-Lytton, on the other hand, inscribed prose of towering majesty and power, a man not afraid of the fanciful phrase nor the deeply held sentiment, a man after my own heart.
Marital Status: Single but Looking

Mrs. Phuddle was now on her date with Mr. Chuckinblaster, defender of all things Bulwer-Lytton. And Mother. Mustn"t forget about Mother.

Arnold Chuckingblaster was a short, plump man with overly long arms, a bushy mustache to match his bushy eyebrows, and sparse head hair. He wore a scowl like a badge of honor, and a rumpled blue suit like Willie Loman.

Mrs. Phuddle wore her navy blue travel pantsuit, in case she needed to make a quick getaway.

They ordered coffee and snacks from the laconic waitress, who sported a most unappetizing nose ring and a snake tattoo writhing around her serving arm.

"So, Mr. Chuckinblaster," Mrs. Phuddle began, as her LockingLips match was busily scowling at his egg salad sandwich. "Tell me a bit about yourself. Ever married?"

His scowl deepened. "No time for such a money sucking venture until now," he grated. "So, how about you, Mrs. Phuddle? Do any weight lifting?" He drew a small notebook from his jacket pocket.

"Umm...no." She sipped her coffee. Instant. "Why do you ask?"

His bushy brows furrowed as he made a small "x" on his notepad. "Would you be willing to take it up? Also, are you a good cook?" He took a giant bite of his sandwich.

Mrs. Phuddle began to see the light, as well as the egg flecks in his mustache. "Er...no, as to the weight lifting. I do a bit of walking and flower tai chi. And I'm a terrible cook!' She crossed her fingers beneath the table.

"Hmmm..." He paused with his questionnaire as the waitress refilled their coffee cups and brought dessert. Mr. Chuckinblaster gobbled up his banana cream pie before Mrs. Phuddle dipped her spoon into her own crème brulee.

"Still, you look sturdy enough," he mused.

Mrs. Phuddle was sipping her coffee, when, to her astonishment, Mr. Chuckinblaster came around behind her chair and began probing with his chubby fingers her shoulders and arms.

Mrs. Phuddle whirled on him like one of those whirling Dervishes. "Sir!" she gasped. "What do you think you're doing?"

He calmly resumed his seat and made a few check marks on his questionnaire. "Just as I thought," he murmured. "Quite sturdy. I bet you're actually a very good cook, too, aren't you?" He chuckled nastily.

Mrs. Phuddle dabbed her lips with a napkin. "Sir, if you're seeking a caretaker for your mother, please refer to the Yellow Pages. Or perhaps there's an app for that."

"What?" he sputtered. "My, what a suspicious mind you have, my dear Mrs. Phuddle."

"I'm not your dear," she retorted. Her only thought now was to pay for her lunch, and get out. Drat that Viola, anyway, she silently fumed. Another one of her bright ideas had gone horribly awry!

"Excuse me, Mrs. Phuddle," her erstwhile date said. "I need to visit the Little Boys' Room."

He headed towards the back of the café. A minute later the waitress presented Mrs. Phuddle with the check. She sat tapping her foot and checking her watch another ten minutes, waiting for Mr. Chuckinblaster to return and pay his share. But she waited in vain.

"That jerk," Mrs. Phuddle muttered, paying the entire bill for lunch. "Wait until I give Viola a piece of my mind!"

Mrs. Phuddle was heading for the exit when Arnold caught up with her, seeming not at all chagrined at stiffing his date for the check.

He peremptorily took her elbow and they walked out the door in tandem.

Mrs. Phuddle shook him loose, glaring icicles from her baby blues.

"Ah, feisty, too," he chortled. 'Mother will like that. She so enjoys a bit of sparring."

"Good day, sir," Mrs. Phuddle primly replied. "And good luck with your future dates. This one is over."

"Didn't you have fun, Geraldine?" he asked smarmily as he caressed the Phuddle shoulder.

"Unhand me, Chuckinblaster!" Mrs. Phuddle exclaimed.

Heads turned on the sidewalk to stare.

"Now, don't make a scene, dear," he cooed, attempting to hook her arm with his.

That did it for our heroine.

Mrs. Phuddle reared back and struck him across his baggy jowls with her handbag.

A few onlookers applauded and cheered.

"You assaulted me!" he yelled as Mrs. Phuddle strode away. "I'll sue you!"

But his witnesses evaporated, as did Mrs. Phuddle. She returned home, made a bracing pot of Earl Grey tea, and hence and forthwith deleted her profile from LockingLips.com.

"Tweet?" Fluffy queried.

"Congratulate me," Mrs. P replied. "I just struck a match."

# Mrs. Phuddle's Celebration Dinners

Mrs. Phuddle does not like to start the New Year with a bang, but rather with black-eyed peas. An old Southern tradition, eating black-eyed peas on New Year's Day supposedly brings good luck. Not one to scoff at Pascal's Wager when it comes to luck, Mrs. Phuddle applies this principle to her NYD's menu:

Mrs. Phuddle's New Year's Day Dinner

Black-eyed peas (duh)
Hot cornbread and butter
Collard greens cooked with ham hock
Onions
Sweet potato pie
Iced tea
~
(Yes, iced tea in the dead of winter!
It's the wine of the South.)

The next big day of celebration on her calendar is St. Valentine's Day, when Mrs. Phuddle's thoughts turn, not only to chocolate, but to hearty French provincial food. For that cold, heartless day in February, Mrs. Phuddle invites her closest friends who usually find themselves still single every February 14th. (Looking at you, Ms. Turgid.)

Mrs. Phuddle's VD Menu

Cassoulet
Crusty French bread
Raspberry sorbet
Chocolate- dipped strawberries
Pink cupcakes
Red, red wine
~
Red roses at table.
Each guest receives one to take home with them.

*

*Faith and begorrah!*

Mrs. Phuddle loves! (So many saints, so little time.) She, of course, wears green on that day and prepares a traditional Irish meal to share with her Celtic friends: Viola O' Turgid, Martha MacFlibber-Gibbet, Lulu O'Sprockett, and on occasion, Petulia MacGoodtimes.

Mrs. Phuddle's St. Patrick's Day Menu

Corned beef and cabbage
Anadama bread
Shamrock cupcakes
Green tea or beer

Anadama bread is made with wheat flour, cornmeal, molasses, and yeast. Easy and delicious! Check your old, decrepit

Betty Cracker cookbooks for the recipe, or if you'd rather, Goggle it. Er...Oogle it?

*

    In the Spring Mrs. Phuddle enjoys a cherry blossom cocktail whilst sitting in her Garden of Earthly Delights at twilight. This pink drink is made with cherry brandy, Triple Sec, lemon juice, and simple syrup. Serve over ice with a cherry on top, or perhaps some mint from your herb garden. You do have an herb garden, don't you?

    For lunch she likes a pimento and cheese sandwich (homemade, natch), or a BLT, washed down with freshly made iced tea.

    In June she starts her day with a blueberry smoothie, a delicious, nourishing concoction of Spooner's Farm Berries, orange juice, yogurt and honey. Frozen blueberries, she finds, work best.

    July is the time for BBQ and ice cream as Independence Day rolls around on the Fourth. Mrs. Phuddle delights in the bounty of this hot summer month and eats, freezes, and cans as much fresh produce as possible.

    Mrs. Phuddle goes into hiding in August, her birthday month, to keep people from asking how old she is. None of their biz! She, Fluffy, and Swimmer hole up in a cozy cabin by Lake Whatnotachuck, where no one can see how much chocolate and ice cream she devours, or how many naps she takes. No one can see, and no one can judge. (Fluffy and Swimmer never judge her.)

And if she spends her evenings watching old Paul Newman movies, who's to know? Only Mrs. Phuddle.

When September rolls around Mrs. Phuddle shops the Farmer's Market for home-grown Washington State apples. She eats them raw, in salads, and makes pies. What's better than apple pie? Almost nothing.

A typical September din-din:

>Meatloaf and gravy
>Mashed potatoes (see gravy, above)
>Green beans (gotta have a green veggies)
>Apple pie

Lunch is so simple in September: Peanut butter and jelly sandwiches, milk and apples. Can't beat it for simplicity and goodness.

October is probably her favorite month! So many good things to enjoy in October:

Hot apple cider with cinnamon sticks
Candied apples
Corn casseroles
Corn chowder
Corn
Pumpkins
Chocolate
Halloween
Autumn leaves…
Melancholy
Sad poetry
The Beast from 10,000 Fathoms

\*

In November Mrs. Phuddle travels to Daisybrook, Georgia, to honor Thanksgiving with her family. The menu is traditional:

>Roast hen or turkey with giblet gravy
>Cornbread dressing—on the side! Not stuffed
>Cranberry sauce
>Squash casserole
>Sweet potato casserole with marshmallows
>Hot rolls
>Pumpkin pie
>Pecan pie

Come December, we find Mrs. Phuddle preparing festive jars of spiced tea as gifts for her friends and neighbors. She includes a batch of Phuddle-made Christmas cookies with every package.

On Christmas Day Mrs. Phuddle lights a few fragrant candles, plays her favorite carols, and serves a lovely dinner for her dearest friends.

Mrs. Phuddle's Christmas Eve Dinner:

>Beef Bourguignon
>Salad with goat cheese, walnuts, and cranberries
>Hot buttery rolls (there's that butter again)

Black Forest Cake
Wine and coffee

Christmas Day is a time of all-day jammies and relaxation with her two beloved animal companions, Fluffy and Swimmer. They both receive special gifts from the pet store, awesome treats, and a lot of love. Mrs. Phuddle sips egg nog, nibbles cookies and opens her own presents, some she received from family in Georgia, some from her friends, and some she buys for herself. And why not?

Later in the day Mrs. Phuddle heats up the wassail and watches an old B&W version of *A Christmas Carol.*

It's the sweetest day of the year.

# A Note from Lindy

I want to thank my beloved husband, Ernie, who has worked so tirelessly to make my dreams come true. Thanks to him, I'm now a published author! Yay!

And another big thank you to my precious Lisa, who inspired me to write these stories long ago, and who so beautifully illustrates the covers of the Mrs. Phuddle Books. One might say Lisa created Mrs. Phuddle, and one might be right.

Also thanks to my dear brother for encouraging me so much by actually reading and enjoying these stories. He seems to really like them! Thank you, Oajz.

And just a special thank-you to all those who read my Mrs. Phuddle stories and seem to love them, including JT, Becca, and Sandy. It means so much to me.

So, at the risk of descending into syrupy sweetness (which Mrs. Phuddle revels in), I just want to add that these little "sweeties" (I dare not call them gems) were written with Love, and given with Love.

I love you all.

Lindy

Made in the USA
Columbia, SC
08 July 2017